WILLIAM MORRIS

This is a Parragon Book
First published in 2001

Parragon
Queen Street House
4 Queen Street
Bath BA1 1HE, UK

ISBN: 0-75254-718-6

A copy of the CIP data for this book is available from
the British Library, upon request.

The right of Iain Zaczek to be identified as the author of this work has been asserted in accordance with Section 77 of the Copyright, Designs and Patents Act of 1988.

The right of Dr Claire I. R. O'Mahoney to be identified as the
author of the introduction to this book has been asserted in accordance with Section
77 of the Copyright, Designs and Patents Act of 1988.

Layout by Essential Books, 7 Stucley Place, London NW1 8NS,
based on an original design by The Foundry Creative Media Company Limited

Printed and bound in Singapore

WILLIAM MORRIS

IAIN ZACZEK

Introduction by Dr Claire I. R. O'Mahony

INTRODUCTION

William Morris was a man of many talents, whose life, and life's work, made a huge impact on the worlds of literature, design and politics. His many ambitions and achievements expressed a profound commitment and belief in an active creative life for all. Morris experimented with every literary genre: prose, political essay, public lecture and poetry. He established the famous design company, Morris and Co., where he enlarged upon the skills he had acquired as an architect to embrace the arts of stained glass, embroidery, wallpaper and furniture design and tapestry. He strove for socialist ideals, both through his various initiatives to create artistic communities inspired by medieval guilds and, in later life, through his writings, lectures and marches working for the socialist cause.

The Morris family, descended from Welsh origins, not only provided an affluent Victorian household in which William developed as a child, but also supported many of his artistic enterprises throughout his life. His parents, William and Emma Morris, had nine children of whom William was the third child and the eldest son to live to maturity. In 1840, his father's successful speculation in a copper mine in Devonshire allowed the family to move from Elm House in Walthamstow to Woodford Hall, a magnificent Palladian villa in Epping Forest.

Morris's idyllic childhood at Woodford Hall was to be a formative influence throughout his life. The house was set in the midst of some of the most picturesque greenery surrounding London and most of his childhood hours were spent discovering its beauties. He inherited his father's fascination for the Middle Ages, which they both indulged through visits to Essex's many parish churches and Canterbury Cathedral; visits to Queen Elizabeth I's hunting lodge at Chingford Hatch awakened the young William to the wonders of traditional English interior decoration. These early experiences instilled an attentive observation of nature in Morris that resonates throughout his wallpaper design and his eloquent evocations of the English countryside in his writings. Morris's childhood medievalism took many forms, from playing on horseback in a miniature suit of armour to reading all of Sir Walter Scott's *Waverley* novels by the age of nine.

Morris's father died in 1848, leaving the family in excellent financial circumstances, but no doubt deeply affected by his loss. Morris was sent to Marlborough College – a new public school for the sons of the emergent Victorian middle class – where he received a classical schooling and learnt to despise the school's haphazard teaching methods. In 1851, after riots at Marlborough, William rejoined his family and completed his secondary education with a private tutor in Walthamstow. The family had resettled there in a Georgian villa, Water House, after his father's death.

While at Marlborough, Morris had discovered the reformative aspirations of the High Church Oxford Movement: in the 1830s a number of leading Anglican theologians in Oxford, most notably John Henry Newman, John Keble and Edward Pusey, had advocated a renewal of piety through more elaborate ceremonial liturgy and a clearer social mission. This movement fascinated Morris and, in 1853, he went up to Exeter College, Oxford. His experiences there – the idyllic medieval city, the circle of idealistic undergraduates and the writings of the Tractarians, Ruskin and Carlyle – were all to shape his artistic, professional and social life.

Edward Burne-Jones, the son of a frame-maker, was also a first-year student at Exeter College; he was to remain Morris's closest friend and artistic collaborator throughout his life. Burne-Jones immediately introduced Morris to his school friends from Birmingham: Charles James Faulkner, Richard Dixon and William Fulford. These young men were all committed students of theology and they discussed the latest ecclesiastical writings and buildings, designed every piece of furniture, glass, tile-work and embroidery and often encouraged the stream of artistic guests to join in the process, creating the ultimate Arts and Crafts collective art work.

The Red House, both because of its costliness and the pleasure and popularity of its innovative design, inspired Morris to create a firm of decorative artists involved in every stage of production. The vogue for improving industrial design set in motion by Prince Albert's patronage of the South Kensington Museum (opened for the tutelage of young designers and craftsmen) and the popularity of Henry Cole's displays at the Great Exhibition of 1851, created the ideal climate for the venture. In the spring of 1861, Morris, Marshall, Faulkner and Co. published a confident prospectus declaring their ambitions to create a new Decorative Art inspired by the skills and integrity of the medieval guilds. P. P. Marshall, a surveyor and sanitary engineer, and Charles Faulkner, who had given up a mathematics fellowship to do the book-keeping, provided the firm's managerial resources. Other non-titular founder members included Burne-Jones, Ford Madox Brown and Rossetti. Many of these artists' female relations also created and executed designs: Kate and Lucy Faulkner and Georgiana Burne-Jones painted ceramics, while Jane Morris and Elizabeth Burden created much of the embroidery.

The potential crisis to which the firm's initial financial disorder might have led was averted by the vogue for medievalism and the patrons it brought to their door. Their work was included in the Medieval Court at the World's Fair, held at South Kensington in 1862, and had a favourable reception. As a result, the firm received its first big commission. G. F. Bodley selected the company to design and make the stained-glass windows for the many churches he had designed in Gloucestershire, Brighton and Scarborough and All Saints' Church and Jesus Chapel in Cambridge. In 1866, the firm received two important private commissions: to decorate every aspect of the Green Dining Room in the South Kensington Museum (now the Victoria and Albert Museum) and the Armoury and Tapestry Rooms at St James's Palace.

The firm strove to provide objects of beauty and utility for every aspect of the home, although stained glass was to be the linchpin of their work in those early years. The vibrant colours which George Campfield and Morris developed were unmatched at the time and, many would argue, since. Philip Webb's furniture, often decorated by Rossetti, Burne-Jones and Morris, was also successful. Morris, who never seemed entirely at ease with depicting the human form, excelled in the design of wallpapers that he described as recreating the charm of the forest inside the home. Messrs Jeffrey and Co. of Islington carved Morris's patterns into pear wood blocks that were then hand-printed.

When Rossetti began to slide into mental instability and Marshall and Faulkner became somewhat apathetic, Morris decided to buy out their shares in the firm for £1,000 each. In 1875, Morris and Co. was formed, with only Burne-Jones, Philip Webb and himself providing the designs. Over the next seven years, Morris was to create the multitude of wallpaper and textile designs for which he is best remembered. The insight of the printers Thomas Clarkson of Preston and Thomas Wardle of Leek were very helpful to Morris in his ambition to create richer colour tonalities by using pre-industrial herbal techniques. Morris also enjoyed experimenting personally with both machine and hand-weaving techniques. The firm complemented their 24 machine-made carpets with a range of hand-woven tapestries worked on a jacquard loom, operated by a silk-weaver from Lyons and an assistant from Spitalfields.

In 1877, the firm opened a shop in Oxford Street, a reflection of its success. A year later, Morris moved into Kelmscott House, an eighteenth-century brick house overlooking the Thames in Hammersmith (leaving Kelmscott Manor, in Oxfordshire for Jane and her lover, Rossetti). Morris hired a number of local women to make the 'Hammersmith' rugs on a carpet loom that he installed in the coach house in the property. As the textile side of the firm's work became their dominant products, Morris and Co. moved its operations to Merton Abbey, a group of buildings originally used for printing, in north Surrey on the River Wandle. By 1887, Morris and Co. had received two royal commissions: to redecorate the throne and reception rooms in St James's Palace and to design a wallpaper for Queen Victoria's new palace at Balmoral in Scotland. This popularity, and the life of comfort in which it allowed Morris to indulge, was to trouble both him and art historians, for it ran counter to his avowed socialist aims of useful and beautiful objects affordable to all.

The medievalism of Morris's youth provided a consistent thread to his political morality of later years, which was so firmly rooted in the Socialism theorised by Karl Marx. Seeking refuge from the romance between his wife and Rossetti, and satisfying a fascination with early Nordic culture, Morris visited Iceland in 1871 and 1873. There he experienced a reawakening of his social conscience when he witnessed the simple dignity of classless life amidst the unrelenting hardships experienced in Reykjavik. It also helped him to imagine a neo-medieval utopian society. Several groups of artists, such as Christopher Dresser's Art Furniture Alliance, Arthur Mackmurdo's Century Guild and C. R. Ashbee's Guild and School of Handicraft, sought to recreate the collective labour of the medieval guild. Morris himself was instrumental in forming the Art Worker's Guild in 1884 and the Art and Craft Exhibition Society in 1886 – key exhibiting venues for these new movements.

Morris joined, and became dissatisfied with, numerous political organisations. He, like Gladstone, Tennyson, Carlyle, Trollope, Darwin and Ruskin, joined the Eastern Question Association, which spoke against the Turkish atrocities in the Bulgarian uprising of 1876. As its treasurer, Morris wrote a letter to the *Daily News* and then a pamphlet entitled *Unjust War: To the Working Men of England*. However, he became disenchanted with the Association, as it became clear that it was largely uninterested in improving the living conditions of the British poor. Morris then became treasurer of The Liberal League that helped to motivate Gladstone's electoral victory in 1880. However, once in office, the Liberal government was to disappoint him as well and once again Morris resigned.

Henry Mayers Hyndman's Social Democrat Federation appeared to express Morris's position more fully, so he joined in 1883. He wrote articles for, and personally distributed, its newspaper *Justice*. When the Federation became beleaguered in the slow process of parliamentary reform, Morris and 10 leaders of its executive formed the Socialist League, one of the strongest advocates for a socialist revolution in 1880s Britain. Few of Morris's friends empathised with his Socialism except Webb and Faulkner, thus he made new friendships, most notably with the Russian émigré anarchist Prince Kropotkin and Friedrich Engels. After the bloodshed on the Bloody Sunday march in 1887 and his removal by the anarchist wing from the editorship of *The Commonweal*, the League's weekly paper, Morris resigned in 1890. He created the Hammersmith Socialist Society, through which he sought to reconcile these two disparate strands of parliamentary and anarchist socialism.

Morris's socialism is most lucid in his writings on art and society. Inspired by a re-reading of Ruskin, Morris became deeply critical of the concept of restoration that allowed for wholesale reconstruction rather than conservation, such as the work of Sir George Gilbert Scott at Tewkesbury Abbey and at Oxford Cathedral. Morris formed The Society for the Protection of Ancient Buildings, known as 'Anti-Scrape' and Morris and Co. refused all further commissions for new stained glass in original medieval churches. During this project, Morris crystallised his socialist theories of the inseverable link between a society and its art, which he set out in *Hopes and Fears of Art* of 1882, an anthology of lectures which he gave in working men's clubs to raise funds for 'Anti-Scrape'. The machine-produced objects of the Victorian age were, according to Morris, ugly and non-functional because they reflected the immoral work practices of the modern factory which alienated the craftsman from his sense of creative satisfaction and were driven by capitalist competition rather than co-operation.

Morris was a prolific writer. *The Oxford and Cambridge Magazine* published his first literary efforts in the 1850s. When Morris, Marshall, Faulkner and Co. was experiencing financial crisis in 1867, Morris returned to writing as a form of escape, producing his epic poem about the search for the Golden Fleece, *The Life and Death of Jason*. This success was followed by his most lengthy and popular poem, *The Earthly Paradise*, of the following year. It recounted 24 legends from every cultural tradition, the East, Iceland and his first love, medieval romance. Morris articulated his socialism not only through his published lectures, but also in his prose works. His Socialist romances *The Pilgrims of Hope* and *The Dream of John Ball* and his futuristic utopian novel *News from Nowhere* appeared in serialised form in *The Commonweal* between 1885 and 1890.

The Kelmscott Press, which printed and bound fine books, grew out of a range of inspirations. Georgiana Burne-Jones, who no doubt provided Morris with great comfort in the 1870s, being aware of the pain of straying marital partners herself, inspired Morris to create some of his most exquisite illuminated manuscripts, *The Book of Verse* and *The Rubaiyat of Omar Khayyam*. Morris had also become fascinated with the Norse legends of Iceland in the 1870s. He met the great Icelandic scholar Eirikr Magnusson in 1862, when he had visited Britain to supervise the publication of a Norse

New Testament and Dictionary. Morris became Magnusson's pupil and the two men went on to collaborate on English translations of *The Saga of Gunnlaug Worm Tongue*, *The Grettis Saga* and *The Volsung Saga*. Morris's first-hand experience of Iceland inspired a saga of his own, *Sigurd the Volsung*, published in 1876. The innovative typography of Nicolas Jensen and the rush of fine art editions produced by new private presses such as Doves and Ashendene encouraged Morris to create the lavishly produced illuminated books that are Kelmscott's greatest achievement.

Initiatives such as the Camden Society, the Early English Text Society and the Chaucer Society had a mission to publish definitive editions of neglected early literature. They had helped to inspire many Victorian writers, such as Sir Alfred Lord Tennyson, for whom Sir Thomas Malory's *Morte d'Arthur* was a vital link in his creation of his epic poem *Idylls of the King*. Kelmscott combined these dual trends of lavish illustration and neglected Early English texts. It published 53 exquisitely illustrated books between 1891 and 1898, the most famous of which is *The Kelmscott Chaucer*, which has 87 woodcuts by Burne-Jones and decorations by Morris.

While Morris and his ideals typify the aspirations and dilemmas of Victorian Britain in microcosm, his importance in shaping twentieth-century culture, both as a critic of its emergent mercantile failings and as a model for its innovators in design, cannot be overestimated. His popularity, which has reached new heights in recent years, reflects the timeless relevance of the man and his thinking.

DR CLAIRE I. R. O'MAHONY

LA BELLE ISEULT (1857–58)

Courtesy of Topham

This is Morris's only surviving oil painting. It depicts his future wife, Jane Burden, in the guise of a tragic Arthurian heroine. Most authorities identify the subject as Iseult, the hapless lover of Tristram, although it has also been seen as a portrait of Guinevere. Both of these themes fascinated Morris. He made preparatory studies for two other pictures of Tristram and Iseult, and drew on the story for the mural he painted in the Oxford Union in 1857. Arthur's queen, meanwhile, inspired many of his early verses, most notably those in *The Defence of Guenevere*, his first volume of poetry, which was published in 1858.

La Belle Iseult is firmly in the Pre-Raphaelite mould – a romantic, medieval subject, executed in a precise, detailed style – but it also highlights Morris's weakness at figure-drawing. The depiction of Jane appears stiff and insipid in comparison with Rossetti's radiant portraits of her. Morris was well aware of this and is said to have scrawled on the canvas, 'I cannot paint you, but I love you'. Despite this, the picture provides an intriguing foretaste of his future artistic direction. Its array of richly patterned textiles and furnishings is reminiscent of the work that was later produced by the Firm.

THE LOVE-LYRICS AND SONGS OF PROTEUS (1892)

Courtesy of the V&A Picture Library

These pages come from the third book to be published by the Kelmscott Press, and are the first not actually written by Morris himself. Despite the apparent simplicity of its design, the book caused Morris a number of major problems. The author, Wilfrid Blunt, insisted on having the large initials printed in red, which complicated the typesetting process considerably. Worse still, part of the text had to be hastily withdrawn and new material added while printing was in progress. Originally, Blunt wanted to open the volume with 'Natalia's Resurrection', a poem alluding to his affair with Margaret Talbot, the wife of an official at the British Embassy in Paris. After she protested vehemently, Blunt had to suppress this section of the book.

Wilfrid Scawen Blunt (1840–1922) was a noted poet and diplomat, and had known Morris for several years. In 1891, he purchased the very first Kelmscott book to come off the presses. His relationship with the artist must have been somewhat strained, however, as he had conducted a prolonged affair with Jane Morris. She proof-read the text of the *Love-Lyrics*, the only occasion on which she was actively involved with production work at the Kelmscott Press.

LXV.

TO ONE WHO SPOKE ILL OF HIM.

WHAT is your quarrel
with me, in Love's
name,
Fair queen of wrath?
What evil have I
done,
What treason to the
thought of our dear
shame
Subscribed or plotted?
Is my heart less one
In its obedience to your stern decrees
Than on the day when first you said, "I please,"
And with your lips ordained our union?
Am I not now, as then, upon my knees?
You bade me love you, and the deed was done,
And when you cried, "Enough," I stopped, and
when
You bade me go I went, and when you said
"Forget me" I forgot. Alas, what wrong
Would you avenge upon a loyal head,
Which ever bowed to you in joy and pain,
That you thus scourge me with your pitiless
tongue?

172

LXVI.

TO ONE WHO HAD LEFT HER
CONVENT TO MARRY.

YEAR ago you gave
yourself to God.
It was a noble gift and
nobly given,
And we who watched
you as you fearless
trod,
Like one inspired,
your pilgrimage to
Heaven,
Rejoiced, poor sinners, there was still this leaven
For a bad world, this bud on Aaron's rod,
This virgin still at watch with the wise seven,
And envying you we almost envied God.
A year ago! Another service now
Moves your delight, another noble whim,
Another bride-groom and another vow.
Again we envy you and envy him,
First God's, then Man's! Your love all ranks
would level.
Who knows? Next year may add a third, the
Devil.

173

19

TITLE-PAGE PROOF FOR THE HISTORY OF REYNARD THE FOXE (1893)

Courtesy of the V&A Picture Library

Morris experimented freely with different colours and styles of ornamentation in his books. For *The History of Reynard the Foxe*, he designed two specimen title-pages, which were engraved by C. E. Keates and then reproduced in red ink. The intention, presumably, was to echo the chapter headings in the main body of the text, which were also printed in red. However, the results were deemed overpowering and the idea was dropped.

The Kelmscott *Reynard* was based on William Caxton's translation of 1481, and was the third Caxton text to be produced by the Press within the space of a year. Morris took great pains to capture the spirit of the original. Early printers had endeavoured to make their books look like illuminated manuscripts – embedding panels of text inside richly decorated borders – and Morris mimicked this effect. With typical thoroughness, he also tried to use similar materials. His paper was made from linen rags and contained no bleaching agent, which ensured that it had the texture and durability of fifteenth-century paper. The Press also issued a few copies of *Reynard* printed on vellum, which were aimed at collectors and sold for 15 guineas apiece.

TITLE-PAGE PROOF FOR THE HISTORY OF REYNARD THE FOXE

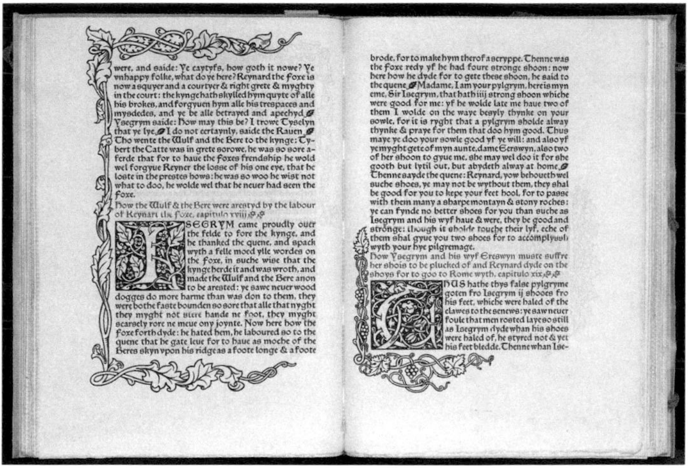

were, and saide: Ye caytyfs, how goth it nowe? Ye vnhappy folke, what do ye here? Reynard the foxe is now a squyer and a courtyer & right grete & myghty in the court: the kynge hath skylled hym quyte of alle his brokes, and forgyuen hym alle his trespaces and mysdedes, and ye be alle betrayed and apechyd. Ysegrym saide: How may this be? I trowe Tyselyn that ye lye. I do not certaynly, saide the Rauen. Tho wente the Wulf and the Bere to the kynge: Tybert the Catte was in grete sorowe, he was so sore aferde that for to haue the foxes frendship he wold wel forgyue Reyner the losse of his one eye, that he loste in the prestes hows: he was so woo he wist not what to doo, he wolde wel that he neuer had seen the foxe.

How the Wulf & the Bere were arestyd by the labour of Reynart the foxe, capitulo xviij.

ISEGRYM came proudly ouer the felde to fore the kynge, and he thanked the quene, and spack wyth a felle moed ylle wordes on the foxe, in suche wise that the kynge herde it and was wroth, and made the Wulf and the Bere anon to be arested: ye sawe neuer wood dogges do more harme than was don to them, they were bothe faste bounden so sore that alle that nyght they myght not stere hande ne foot, they myght scarsely rore ne meue ony joynte. Now here how the foxe forth dyde: he hated hem, he laboured so to the quene that he gate leue for to haue as moche of the Beres skyn vpon his ridge as a foote longe & a foote

brode, for to make hym therof a scryppe. Thenne was the foxe redy yf he had foure stronge shoon: now here how he dyde for to gete these shoon, he said to the quene. Madame, I am your pylgrym, here is myn eme, Sir Isegrym, that hath iiij strong shoon whiche were good for me: yf he wolde late me haue two of them I wolde on the waye besyly thynke on your sowle, for it is ryght that a pylgrym sholde alway thynke & praye for them that doo hym good. Thus maye ye doo your sowle good yf ye will: and also yf ye myght gete of myn aunte, dame Eerswyn, also two of her shoon to gyue me, she may wel doo it for she gooth but lytil out, but abydeth alway at home. Thenne sayde the quene: Reynard, yow behoueth wel suche shoes, ye may not be wythout them, they shal be good for you to kepe your feet hool, for to passe with them many a sharpe montayn & stony roches: ye can fynde no better shoes for you than suche as Isegrym and his wyf haue & were, they be good and stronge: though it sholde touche their lyf, eche of them shal gyue you two shoes for to accomplyssh wyth your hye pilgremage.

How Ysegrym and his wyf Ereswyn muste suffre her shois to be plucked of and Reynard dyde on the shoys for to goo to Rome wyth, capitulo xix.

THUS hathe thys false pylgryme goten fro Isegrym ij shooes fro his feet, whiche were haled of the clawes to the senews: ye saw neuer foule that men rosted laye so still as Isegrym dyde whan his shoes were haled of, he styred not & yet his feet bledde. Thenne whan Ise-

THE STORY OF THE GLITTERING PLAIN (1891)

Courtesy of the V&A Picture Library

These pages come from the first book published by the Kelmscott Press. Initially, Morris had intended to embark on his 'little typographical adventure' by producing a new edition of Caxton's *Golden Legend*. This proved to be a slow and complicated undertaking, however, so instead Morris opted for a less ambitious project. He reprinted one of his own tales, *The Story of the Glittering Plain*, which had originally been published in the *English Illustrated Magazine* (1890). This appeared in print in May 1891. Three years later, Morris produced a more lavish second edition, featuring 23 illustrations by Walter Crane.

The Glittering Plain was set in Morris's first type-face, the Golden type. He based this on the lettering of two fifteenth-century books, Nicolas Jenson's *Pliny* (1476) and Rubeus's edition of Aretino's *Historia Florentina* (1476). His friend, Emery Walker, made photographic enlargements of several pages from these texts. Morris then traced out individual characters and remodelled them to form his own designs. At first, he was going to call the results the 'Jenson-Morris' type, but settled on 'Golden' type in honour of the *Golden Legend* project.

CHAPTER XIII. HALLBLITHE BE-
HOLDETH THE WOMAN WHO
LOVETH HIM.

UT on the morrow the
men arose, and the Sea-
eagle & his damsel came
to Hallblithe; for the
other two damsels were
departed, and the Sea-
eagle said to him: "Here
am I well honoured and
measurelessly happy; &
I have a message for
thee from the King. ⟨ "What is it?" said
Hallblithe; but he deemed that he knew what
it would be, and he reddened for the joy of
his assured hope. ⟨ Said the Sea-eagle: "Joy
to thee, O shipmate! I am to take thee to the
place where thy beloved abideth, and there shalt
thou see her, but not so as she can see thee;
and thereafter shalt thou go to the King, that
thou mayst tell him if she shall accomplish thy
desire." ⟨ Then was Hallblithe glad beyond
measure, and his heart danced within him, and
he deemed it but meet that the others should
be so joyous and blithe with him, for they led
him along without any delay, and were glad at
his rejoicing; and words failed him to tell of his
gladness. ⟨ But as he went, the thoughts of his
coming converse with his beloved curled sweetly

86

round his heart, so that scarce anything had
seemed so sweet to him before; and he fell a-
pondering what they twain, he & the Hostage,
should do when they came together again; whether they should abide on the Glittering Plain
or go back again to Cleveland by the Sea and
dwell in the House of the Kindred; and for his
part he yearned to behold the roof of his fathers
and to tread the meadow which his scythe had
swept, and the acres where his hook had smitten
the wheat. But he said to himself, "I will wait
till I hear her desire hereon."
⟨ Now they went into the wood at the back of
the King's pavilion and through it and so over
the hill, and beyond it came into a land of hills
and dales exceeding fair and lovely; and a river
wound about the dales, lapping in turn the feet
of one hill-side or the other; and in each dale (for
they passed through two) was a goodly house
of men, and tillage about it, and vineyards and
orchards. They went all day till the sun was
near setting, and were not weary, for they turned into the houses by the way when they would,
and had good welcome, and meat & drink, and
what they would of the folk that dwelt there.
Thus anigh sunset they came into a dale fairer
than either of the others, and nigh to the end
where they had entered it was an exceeding
goodly house. Then said the damsel: ⟨ "We
are nigh-hand to our journey's end; let us sit

87

TITLE-PAGE DESIGN FOR THE STORY OF THE GLITTERING PLAIN (1894)

Courtesy of the V&A Picture Library

This is the only book which was brought out in two editions by the Kelmscott Press. At the time of the first printing (1891), Morris had enquired about the possibility of illustrations, but had been too impatient to wait for them. This second edition, however, was published in a larger format and featured 23 woodcut illustrations by Walter Crane. Although Crane was famed for his work as a children's illustrator, Morris and his colleagues were disappointed with the results. Philip Webb commented, 'the book is quite up to the mark in all but the pictures ... However, do not mind – the whole book looks delightful; and, for the pictures ... why, they are more than helped out by the borders'. Crane was equally conscious of the problem, doubting 'if I was ever quite Gothic enough in feeling to suit his [Morris's] taste'.

The finished title-page was modelled closely on the design seen here. However, Morris decided that the letter 'i' in 'Plain' and the two characters immediately below it created an unsightly vertical emphasis on the page. Accordingly, the spacing between the words was altered slightly in the printed version.

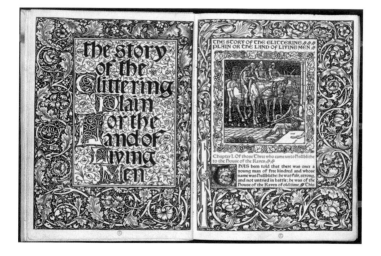

DESIGN FOR INITIAL WORD (1896)

Courtesy of the V&A Picture Library

In a letter to William and Jane's daughter, May Morris, Sydney Cockerell explained how the earliest designs for initials and borders were made. 'Your father had two little saucers in front of him. He roughed out his design in pencil – then drew it again carefully with his black brush, correcting with white and then again with black as he went on, and using white over the black for various little details...' Morris's favourite colour combination, used both here and in the title-page design for *The Glittering Plain* (1891), was blue ink and Chinese white. Morris's designs were then redrawn by Robert Catterson-Smith (later the Head of the Birmingham School of Art) and transferred photographically to the woodblock. The final engraving was executed by William Hooper.

This is one of many designs that were used in the preparation of *The Works of Geoffrey Chaucer* (1896). It is the opening word ('Whilom', meaning 'Once') of 'The Knight's Tale'. As usual, Catterson-Smith interpreted Morris's drawing with extreme sensitivity, and the final, printed version appears identical to the naked eye.

PROOF FOR FROISSART'S CHRONICLES (C. 1895)

Courtesy of the V&A Picture Library

Froissart's *Chronicles* had been one of Morris's favourite books ever since his Oxford days, and he had long cherished the idea of producing a new edition for the Kelmscott Press. The first trial page was laid out in 1892, as soon as the Troy type was available, and further test pages followed at regular intervals. In part, the delays were caused by the workload attached to the Chaucer, though the real problem was the scale of Morris's ambition. The *Chronicles*, which covered the period of the Hundred Years' War, epitomised for him all the romance and glamour of the Middle Ages. Morris wished to convey this by designing some amazingly elaborate borders, densely packed with coats of arms and intertwining foliage. Here, he has sketched in a few preliminary ideas for the border in pencil. However, the page was subsequently re-set so he could incorporate larger initials and a more complex border into his design.

Sadly, the *Chronicles* remained unfinished at Morris's death, and the project was eventually abandoned. Sixteen-page samples of the text were printed and distributed to the artist's friends. These were warmly received. Swinburne, for example, wrote back to Cockerell saying, 'a thousand thanks for your beautiful and precious gift. Why did not Morris take up and finish Froissart earlier…'.

PIGSKIN BINDING FOR THE WORKS OF GEOFFREY CHAUCER (1896)

Courtesy of the Syndics of Cambridge University Library

Most of the books published by the Kelmscott Press were produced in two formats: standard and deluxe. For the *Chaucer*, the most elaborate of all his publications, Morris went even further. The deluxe editions were to be printed on vellum and were to have a choice of four special bindings: a full or half pigskin produced at the Doves Bindery, or a different full or half pigskin designed by Frederic, Lord Leighton. In the end, however, only the Doves' full pigskin design appears to have been used, although there is a dummy copy of the book in the Leighton binding at Columbia University.

The sumptuous design of the cover was modelled closely on a bible produced by Ulrich Schreier in 1478. This is particularly evident from the lozenges and oak-leaf patterns in the central panel. Surrounding this, the inner border contains heavily stylised vine leaves, which are meant to echo the more naturalistic versions inside the book. Morris was very happy with the results and planned to use a similar binding on his Froissart's *Chronicles*. He told an interviewer, 'it will be in white pigskin – a beautiful material for wearing and showing designs...'. One of the pigskin copies of the *Chaucer* was later owned by Lawrence of Arabia.

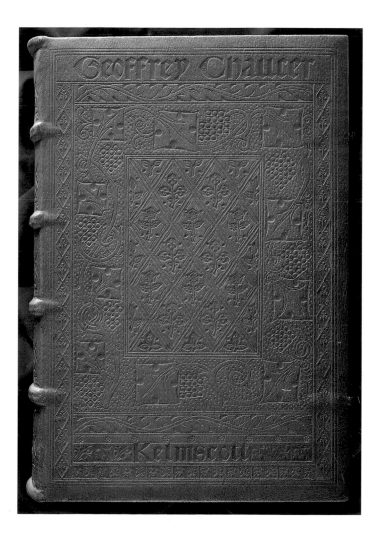

Proof from The Works of Geoffrey Chaucer (1896)

Courtesy of the V&A Picture Library

One of the highlights of the Kelmscott *Chaucer* was the fruitful collaboration between Morris and Burne-Jones. The latter produced 87 illustrations for the text (a huge increase on the 40 which had originally been envisaged) and these were set in 18 different frames, designed by Morris. On this proof, he produced an experimental version of one of these borders, working in Indian ink and Chinese white.

Burne-Jones was delighted with the decorative frames, declaring that he 'loved to be snugly cased in borders and buttressed up by the vast initials ... if you drag me out of my encasings, it will be like tearing a statue out of its niche and putting it in a museum'. He was less happy, however, with Morris's entreaties that he should tackle some of the bawdier tales. 'Morris has been urgent with me that I should by no means exclude these stories from our scheme of adornment – especially he had hopes of my treatment of the Miller's Tale.' In this picture, however, Burne-Jones illustrated one of the tamer narratives, *The Tale of the Clerk of Oxenford*. This dealt with the tribulations of patient Griselda (second from left) and, as in his *Adoration* (1887–1906), the scene is set against a background of plain wickerwork and foliage.

NEWS FROM NOWHERE (1893)

Courtesy of the V&A Picture Library

This strange, Utopian novel is Morris's best-known prose work. It was serialised in *The Commonweal* in 1890 and published in book-form by Reeves & Turner in 1891. The Kelmscott edition of the tale was completed in November 1892. It was printed in Golden type and included a number of Morris's decorated borders and initials. Its most familiar feature is the accompanying illustration of Kelmscott Manor, Morris's Oxfordshire home. This was engraved by Hooper, after a drawing by Charles Gere. Three hundred copies of the book were printed, along with ten copies produced on vellum.

The novel provides a colourful interpretation of Morris's political convictions. In it, the author awakes one morning in his Hammersmith home, to find that he has been transported to the early twenty-first century, when all his socialist aspirations have come true. London has been transformed; its factories have been swept away, along with all the trappings of capitalism and industrialism. Hammersmith Bridge is decked out more attractively than the Ponte Vecchio, while the Houses of Parliament are used as a dung market. Morris's imaginary tour continues with a trip up the Thames, culminating in his arrival at Kelmscott Manor during the hay-making season.

THIS IS THE PICTURE OF THE OLD HOUSE BY THE THAMES TO WHICH THE PEOPLE OF THIS STORY WENT. HEREAFTER FOLLOWS THE BOOK IT SELF WHICH IS CALLED NEWS FROM NOWHERE OR AN EPOCH OF REST & IS WRITTEN BY WILLIAM MORRIS.

NEWS FROM NOWHERE OR AN EPOCH OF REST. CHAPTER I. DISCUSSION AND BED.

UP at the League, says a friend, there had been one night a brisk conversational discussion, as to what would happen on the Morrow of the Revolution, finally shading off into a vigorous statement by various friends, of their views on the future of the fully-developed new society.

SAYS our friend: Considering the subject, the discussion was good-tempered; for those present, being used to public meetings & after-lecture debates, if they did not listen to each other's opinions, which could scarcely be expected of them, at all events did not always attempt to speak all together, as is the custom of people in ordinary polite society when conversing

THE ROOTS OF THE MOUNTAINS (1890)

Courtesy of the V&A Picture Library/John Dreyfus

Morris was concerned that his books should be admired as physical objects, not purely for the quality of their writing. 'I began printing books,' he declared, 'with the hope of producing some which would have a definite claim to beauty.' Even prior to his involvement with the Kelmscott Press, Morris did his utmost to achieve this within the constraints of the conventional publishing world. At the Chiswick Press, for example, he designed three of his own books, hoping to give them something of an incunabular air. Both *The House of the Wolfings* (1889) and *The Roots of the Mountains* were printed in Basle Roman, one of the few old typefaces that was still commercially available. A special edition of the latter was also printed on high-quality Whatman paper and bound in block-printed linen from Merton Abbey. Two different patterns were employed: Little Chintz or, as here, Honeysuckle.

Morris was almost indecently happy with the results. 'I am so pleased with my book – typography, binding and, must I say it, literary matter – that I am any day to be seen huggling it up, and am becoming a spectacle to Gods and men because of it.' A copy of the book was displayed at the 1890 Arts and Crafts Exhibition.

THE STORY OF HEN-THORIR (C. 1874)

Courtesy of the Bodleian Library

Morris's long-standing fascination with Icelandic literature took a positive turn in 1868, when he began studying the language under the leadership of Eirikr Magnusson. His ultimate aim was to translate some of the sagas in order to enable the Victorian public to become acquainted with this forgotten landmark of northern culture. 'This is the great story of the North,' he said of the *Volsunga Saga*, 'which should be to all our race what the *Tale of Troy* was to the Greeks.' Morris translated *The Story of Hen-Thorir* in collaboration with Magnusson, and reproduced it in manuscript form on more than one occasion. Along with *The Story of the Banded-Men* and *The Story of Haward the Halt*, he first included it in the volume of *Icelandic Stories*, which he produced as a gift for Georgiana Burne-Jones. Her initials figure prominently amid the decoration on the title page. In 1909, she donated it to the Fitzwilliam Museum in Cambridge with this inscription: 'the three stories in this book were translated from the Icelandic by W. Morris and Eirikr Magnusson. They were written out, and all the illuminated letters were designed and painted by W. Morris, about the year 1873. He then gave the book to me, and I now give it to the Fitzwilliam Museum in memory of him.'

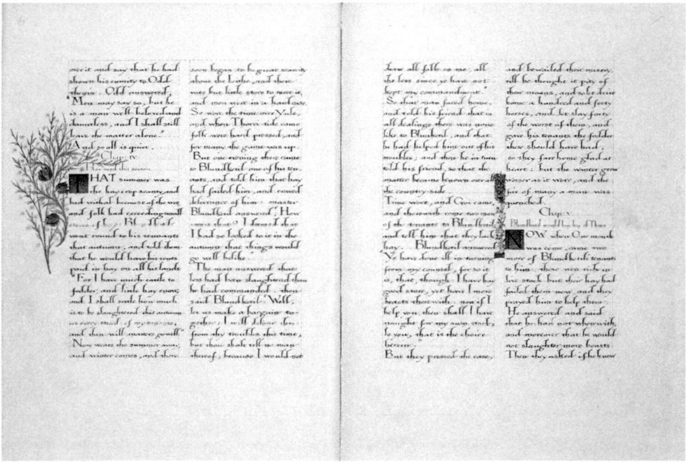

THE WELL AT THE WORLD'S END (1896)

Courtesy of the V&A Picture Library

This project was bedevilled with production problems. Before the end of 1892, the text had been prepared, the borders designed and trial pages had been printed. Despite this, the book was not actually issued until the summer of 1896. The main problem lay with the illustrations, which were originally entrusted to Arthur Gaskin (1862–1928), a prominent artist and illustrator from Birmingham. He submitted a total of 19 different designs, but all were refused by Morris, who turned to his old friend Burne-Jones for the four woodcuts that appeared in the published version of the book. The reason for the rejection of Gaskin's designs was never specified, but it may have been a matter of Morris's personal taste. Later Gaskin was hired to produce illustrations for another Kelmscott Press publication, *The Shepheardes Calender*, issued shortly after Morris's death.

The Well at the World's End was Morris's final prose romance, telling the story of Prince Ralph, who set out on a quest to find the fabled well, which could confer eternal youth upon those who drank from its waters. The tale is unfashionable today, but it appealed to contemporaries and received a glowing review from W. B. Yeats.

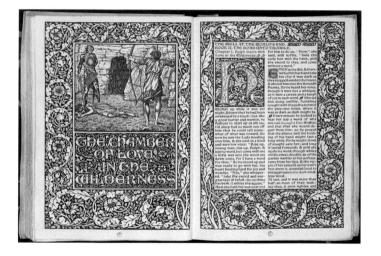

THE RUBAIYAT OF OMAR KHAYYAM (1872)

Courtesy of the British Library

It is hardly surprising that Morris should have chosen to tackle this popular book, as *The Rubaiyat* was one of the great success stories of Victorian publishing. It was translated into English by the Suffolk poet, Edward FitzGerald, and the first edition appeared in 1859. This did not sell particularly well, but it was greatly admired by Rossetti and, partly as a result of his enthusiasm, a second edition was brought out in 1868. The book also proved popular with the other Pre-Raphaelites, who revelled in its hedonistic message of a life devoted to pleasure and beauty.

Morris transcribed the poems in a neat Roman minuscule, probably with a crow-quill pen. He also illuminated the text, using a prolific amount of gilding to conjure up an air of oriental opulence. This spread, which appears at the end of the volume, is one of the most lavish of all. Morris embarked on four separate copies of the manuscript, although he only completed one, presenting it to Georgiana Burne-Jones. This was not unusual; one of his colleagues once said with regret: 'Morris will start half a dozen jobs; he has designs for perhaps half of them, and therefore in a week or two they have to be given up. They are put away, bits get lost, have to be done over again; hence a great loss of time and money.'

My threadbare penitence apieces tore.

71

And much as wine has played the infidel,
And robbed me of my robe of honour — well,
I often wonder what the vintners buy
One half so precious as the goods they sell.

72

Alas, that Spring should vanish with the rose,
That Youth's sweet-scented manuscript should
The Nightingale that in the branches sang
Ah whence, and whither flown again, who knows!

73

Ah Love! could thou and I with Fate conspire
To grasp this sorry scheme of things entire,
Would we not shatter it to bits, and then
Remould it nearer to the heart's desire?

Ah Moon of my delight who knowest no wane,
The Moon of Heaven is rising once again:
How oft hereafter rising shall she look
Through this same garden after me — in vain.

75

And when Thyself with shining foot shall pass
Among the guests star-scattered on the grass,
And in thy joyous errand reach the spot
Where I made one — turn down an empty glass!

THE BROTHERS GRIMM (1857)

Courtesy of Sir Paul Getty, KBE, the Wormsley Library

The majority of Morris's manuscripts were produced between 1870 and 1875, during a period of intense artistic activity. Before this, however, he had made a number of other, sporadic attempts in the field. There is, for example, this single-page specimen, which features part of a story by the Brothers Grimm (*The Iron Man*). It dates back to 1857, when the artist was just 23 years old, and clearly betrays the influence of his recent student days. While he was at Oxford (1853–55), Morris was a regular visitor to the Bodleian Library, where he was able to pore over early manuscripts at his leisure.

Morris later dismissed this work as a piece of juvenilia, recognising that it was little more than a pastiche. It contained the sort of elements that he would later leave to other hands, such as the historiated initial and miniature heads. On the other hand, there were other areas where he would improve beyond all measure. Set beside these clumsy stylisations, the floral motifs in his mature work appear supremely naturalistic. Interestingly, the page confirms that some of Morris's working methods were developed at a very early stage. The partly-erased sketches in the right-hand margin suggest that he always preferred designing his borders on the page, rather than working them out separately.

ow there was once a king that lived merrily, and above all things as he loved hunting no here befell him great tribulation: for one day when divers of his great lords

held him in the hall divers others went forth to hunt: who came not back again that night or any night, either lords or poor folk

either did those who went to seek them come back how many so ever years passed: so no man dared enter that forest till at last a certain came into that land who said that he would achieve the adventure or die ... council

strong wood and to lock up therein the wild man, nor did they ever suffer him to come out; and at first the people pelted him with stones and mud and cabbages but at last getting tired of him let him alone

the king had a young son who one day played at ball in the oven quadrangle of the palace wherein also the cage of the wild man was; and as he played his gold ball roll ed away into the cage whereon the prince prayed him heartily to give him the ball again, nay said the wild man will you open the door of my cage; I cannot said the child, and went away sorrowfully

at the next day when both the king was out and the Queen, the boy came and stood pensively by the cage where the wild man was sitting, smiling kindly to himself

when he saw the prince he called out to him: So you have come for your ball again, well you know the key lies under the Queens pillow, let me out and then for the ball

ud it did not warm him much that as he passed long streets the go out of gates, the young men wagged their heads to each other and laughed, or that the old men wagged their heads and looked wise and muttered, no not even that many of the women wept

ut it was because he had lost his love ... he passed into the forest with his hounds and a little while out of them seeing a wild beast over chase to it, but presently chancing to cross some water, a great rusty brown naked hand and arm rose and dragged the dog down under the water then the hunter said what had happened to those missing huntsmen, and he caused the county people to take all the water out of that pool, and when this was done beheld they lay a great wild man rusty-brown and naked who moaned when they bound him

therefore the prince fetched the key and opened the cage door. So then the wild man when he felt himself free threw up his arms and shouted, and began to stride off: But the prince cried out after him to stop or that he should be beaten for letting him go.

whereupon he caught and turning took the prince in his arms and ran away with him into the forest where they dwelt together for years and years till the prince had almost forgotten who he was at last one day the iron man took him to a place where there was a pool of wa ... and said to him:

... you hold this pool till you see its brightest crystal you must not let anything fall in so should not live it, for they it will be disdonia ured?

... the prince watched and for some time things went well enough till at last the extra sore

this way the knight brought to the King and then departed with many gifts and much honour.

... them to make ... the King caus a cage of iron and

pain in one finger so that he could not refrain from dipping it into the water.

THE STORY OF FRITHIOF THE BOLD
(C. 1873)

Courtesy of Sir Paul Getty, KBE, the Wormsley Library

It is no accident that several of Morris's manuscripts dealt with Icelandic themes, for the place was uppermost in his thoughts during the early 1870s. His first trip there took place in the summer of 1871, just after his wife and Rossetti ensconced themselves in Kelmscott Manor, and it may have been intended as a distraction from the collapse of his marriage. Once the expedition was under way, however, Morris became totally immersed in the experience. He admired the stoicism of the people – Iceland was one of the poorest countries in Europe – and marvelled at the spectacle of a land that was still apparently untainted by capitalism and industrialism. 'A most beautiful and poetical place it seemed to me,' he wrote in his journal, 'it looked as if ... the old life of the saga-time had gone, and the modern life had never reached the place.' It was this mixture of primitive power and innocence that he sought to capture in his Icelandic works.

Morris transcribed the main text of *Frithiof* and planned out the framework of the decoration, but he left most of its execution to other hands. Fairfax Murray painted the vignette scenes and the large initials, while Louise Powell was responsible for the trailing bands of flowers. The gilded running heads and remaining initials were provided by Graily Hewitt.

CHAP. XIII.

NOW weareth away the mid-winter, and when spring cometh, the weather groweth fair, the wood bloometh, the grass groweth, and ships may glide betwixt land and land.

So on a day the king says to his folk: "I will that ye come with us for our disport out into the woods, that we may look upon the fairness of the earth."

So did they, and went flock-meal with the king into the woods: but so it befell, that the king and Frithiof were gotten alone together afar from other men, and the king said he was heavy, and would fain sleep; then said Thief: Get thee home, then, lord, for it better beseemeth men of high estate to lie at home than abroad.

"Nay," said the king "so will I not do." And he laid him down there-with, and slept fast, snoring loud. Thief sat close by him, and presently drew his sword from his sheath, & cast it far away from him.

A little while after the king woke up, and said: "Was it not so, Frithiof, that a many things came into thy mind e'en now? but well hast thou dealt with them, and great honour shalt thou have of me. Lo now, I knew thee straightway, that first evening thou camest into our hall: now nowise speedily shalt thou de-part from us, and somewhat great abideth thee."

Said Frithiof: "Lord king, thou hast done to me well, and in friendly wise; but yet must I get me gone soon, because my company cometh speedily to meet me, as I have given them charge to do."

So then they rode home from the wood, and the king's folk came flocking to him, and home they fared to the hall and drank joyously; and it was made known to all folk that Frithiof the Bold had been abiding there through the winter-tide.

CHAP. XIV.

EARLY of a morning-tide one smote on the door of that hall, wherein slept the king and queen, and many others: then the king asked who it was that called at the hall door; and so he who was without said: "Here am I, Frithiof, and I am arrayed for my departure."

Then was the door opened, and Frithiof came in, and sang a stave:

Have great thanks for the guesting
Thou gavest with all bounty;
Dight fully for departure
Is the eagles' feeder now;
But Ingibiorg I mind thee,
While yet on earth I dwell,
Live gloriously! I give thee
This gift for many kisses

FOUR PINK AND HAWTHORN TILES (1887)

Courtesy of the V&A Picture Library

There is an element of uncertainty about the attribution of this tile design. When William de Morgan's widow bequeathed a large collection of archive material to the Victoria and Albert Museum in 1917, she included three sets of papers relating to Morris. One of these, dating back to 1887, cites a Morris *Pink and Hawthorn* design, which has been tentatively linked with these tiles. It is unclear, however, whether the original design was created by Morris himself, or whether it was a de Morgan tile produced for the Firm. Stylistically, it is much closer to de Morgan's work; indeed, both in format and colouring, it is almost identical to the *Carnations and Primroses* design which he was still selling in 1898.

William de Morgan enjoyed a long association with Morris and his circle. He first became interested in the ideals of the Pre-Raphaelites while still a student at the Royal Academy Schools, in the early 1860s. He met Morris in 1863, just a year after the latter had started designing his own tiles, and was soon producing work for the Firm.

TULIP AND TRELLIS TILE (1870)

Courtesy of the V&A Picture Library

Morris's association with de Morgan was a complex affair. For the latter, at least, it was also a highly sensitive issue. 'A common error,' he once remarked, 'is to suppose that I was a partner in Morris's firm. I was never connected with his business beyond the fact that, on his own initiative, he exhibited and sold my work, and that subsequently he employed my tiles in his schemes of decoration.' Certainly de Morgan retained his independence, although his ceramic works were never very far away from the Firm. Prior to 1872, he worked in Fitzroy Square before moving to Cheyne Row in Chelsea (1872–81). He then transferred his workshops to Merton Abbey (1882–88), before finally settling at the Sands End Pottery in Fulham (1888–97).

In spite of his protests, de Morgan did occasionally make use of Morris designs. He would admit to only three, however, including this particular design. In a conversation with his sister-in-law he stated, 'Morris never made but three designs for my execution, the *Tulip and Trellis*, the *Poppy* and another – I forget the name. I never could work except by myself and in my own manner.'

TILES FOR MEMBLAND PANEL (1876)

Courtesy of the V&A Picture Library

This is one of a set of six panels which were commissioned by the architect George Devey for Membland Hall in Devon, the home of banking magnate E. C. Baring. The artist's design has survived, together with a set of instructions, which confirm that the panels were destined for the bathroom. They remained in situ until 1928, when Membland Hall was demolished.

This was the largest and most complex of the floral patterns that Morris designed for use in a tile panel. Perhaps because of this, he had reservations about producing the tiles himself. Instead, he contracted de Morgan's company to provide them. This was a logical step, since de Morgan had a special gift for assimilating large-scale tile designs into architectural settings. His most famous scheme, the Arab Hall at Lord Leighton's house, dates from around this period. Morris & Co. continued to advertise the pattern on its stocklists until as late as 1913, and the creation of several similar panels is documented in their order books. Later examples were hand-painted on de Morgan's own tiles, produced at his Sands End Pottery in Fulham, while the Membland Hall panels were executed on blank, earthenware tiles supplied by the Architectural Pottery in Poole.

IMAGO PHYLLIDIS MARTYRIS (C. 1870)

Courtesy of the V&A Picture Library

This is one of a series of tile panels that were based on subjects from Chaucer's poem 'Legend of Good Women'. This figure, designed by Burne-Jones, is Phyllis, a mythical queen of Thrace. She fell in love with Demophoön, the son of Theseus, but he abandoned her. She then attempted suicide but was turned into an almond tree by Athene. Eventually, Demophoön returned to Thrace and heard of the tragedy. Stricken with guilt, he embraced the tree, which suddenly burst into blossom. Phyllis then reappeared from within the tree trunk. Burne-Jones tackled this dramatic moment in one of his most controversial paintings, *Phyllis and Demophoön* (1870), but here the incident is conveyed by the sprig of almond blossom that Phyllis holds in her hand.

Originally, Burne-Jones conceived this figure as part of a stained-glass design and used it to decorate the windows at Birket Foster's house. The present arrangement, where the figure forms part of a tile panel, was in general use by Morris, Marshall, Faulkner & Co. during the late 1860s and early 1870s. The border is composed of blue-and-white Scroll tiles, a pattern which was frequently used in Victorian fireplaces. This particular panel was one of a pair, which were installed at the London home of the Earl of Carlisle.

CHAUCER TILE (1863)

Courtesy of the V&A Picture Library

The medieval tastes of the Pre-Raphaelite circle were not confined to art, but also extended to literature. Chaucer was a favourite author and Ford Madox Brown, for example, was composing paintings on Chaucerian themes from the mid-1840s. Both Morris and Burne-Jones became fascinated with the poet during their student days, and his verses provided a constant source of inspiration for them throughout their careers. Chaucerian subjects featured in paintings, tapestries, stained glass and books.

This stylish portrait was designed by Burne-Jones in 1863 and copied on to a tile by Morris in the following year. The model is thought to have been Rossetti. Originally, the portrait was designed for a stained-glass roundel at the home of the illustrator Myles Birket Foster. Morris, Marshall, Faulkner & Co. carried out this commission in 1862–64. The tile later passed into the hands of Professor Arthur Church, an authority on ceramics at the South Kensington Museum (now the Victoria and Albert Museum). He inscribed on the back of the frame, 'very few of the tiles subsequently issued by Morris & Co. appear to have been painted by Morris himself, but ... Mr Morris told me with respect to this tile that he painted it himself'.

EMBROIDERED SCREEN WITH THREE HEROINES (C. 1860)

Courtesy of the Castle Howard Collection

This is the most substantial surviving section of the drawing-room decorations in the Red House. Initially, Morris envisaged a series of 12 vertical hangings depicting famous heroines. These were loosely based on the 'martyrs to love' in Chaucer's 'Legend of Good Women'. This particular trio has been identified as Lucretia, Hippolyte and Helen of Troy. According to legend, Lucretia was the virtuous wife of Tarquinius Collatinus. After being raped by Sextus, the son of the king of Rome, she informed her husband, urging him to seek vengeance, and then committed suicide. She is shown here holding the sword with which she stabbed herself. Hippolyte, the central figure, was the Amazon queen who fell in love with Hercules but was defeated by him. In some versions of the legend, she married Theseus and became the Queen of Athens. Helen of Troy was abducted by Paris, son of King Priam of Troy. Her husband, Menelaus of Sparta, fought to reclaim her, thus beginning the Trojan War.

The Red House scheme was not finished and the various panels were eventually dispersed. These three appear to have been shown at the 1888 Arts and Crafts Exhibition by Bessie Burden, Morris's sister-in-law. In the following year, she sold them to George Howard for £80.

DESIGN FOR AN EMBROIDERED PANEL (C. 1860)

Courtesy of the V&A Picture Library

This delicate drawing, executed in pencil and watercolour, was a preliminary study for one of the embroidered hangings in the Red House. It depicts Helen, the tragic wife of Menelaus. In her hand, she holds a blazing torch with a scroll which identifies her as 'the Flame of Troy'. The panels were intended to decorate the drawing room of the Red House, and the bulk of the work was to be carried out by the wives and friends of the Pre-Raphaelites. In the main, these consisted of Jane Morris, her sister Bessie, Georgiana Burne-Jones and Kate Faulkner. As so often, Morris's concept proved over-ambitious: he favoured a complicated, late-medieval technique, which involved embroidering the figures on linen and transferring them to a heavy silk background. His timing was equally unfortunate, because Jane – the most skilful needlewoman of the group – was extremely busy looking after their two young children.

Helen was one of the few figures in the series to be completed. It was embroidered by Bessie Burden and joined with two other panels to form the decorative screen now in the Castle Howard Collection.

FIGURE OF GUINEVERE (C. 1860)

Courtesy of the Tate Gallery

This is one of several extant studies for a series of embroidered hangings which were to decorate the drawing room in the Red House. In theory, the 12 figures were meant to be drawn from Chaucer's 'Legend of Good Women', but Morris only used this as a starting point. Guinevere was featured as she fitted in with the general theme of 'martyrs to love', even though she had not figured in Chaucer's poem.

The series was never completed, but several other preparatory works are known. These include two partly-finished embroidered panels depicting Phyllis (another of the heroines) and a pomegranate tree. There is also a notebook containing sketches which show how the finished scheme might have looked. Among other things, it indicates that there were plans to incorporate the figure of Chaucer himself into the scheme.

The 'Legend of Good Women' was to prove a popular theme with both Morris and Burne-Jones, and several other versions of the subject are known. Burne-Jones designed a series of tiles on the subject for J. R. Spencer Stanhope's house (1862) and the Firm also marketed tiled panels of Phyllis and Philomela. In addition, Burne-Jones designed a second series of embroidered panels which were to be executed by the girls of Winnington Hall School in Cheshire.

EMBROIDERED HANGING (EARLY 1860s)

Courtesy of Christie's Images

This unusual specimen is one of a set of four embroidered hangings which were on display at Penskill Castle in Ayrshire. This was the home of Alice Boyd, the mistress of William Bell Scott, an artist who was closely associated with the Pre-Raphaelite circle. It was presumably through this connection that the hangings were acquired, although Scott may not have admired them personally. His initial reaction to the Red House decorations was somewhat mixed; 'the total effect was strange and barbaric to Victorian sensibility,' he commented, 'and the adornment had a novel, not to say, startling character...' Nevertheless, the hangings were in place by 1868, when Rossetti referred to the 'Topsaic tapestries' ('Topsy' was Morris's nickname) in a letter.

The style of the embroidery, with its repeated motto – *Qui bien aime tard oublie* (he who loves well is slow to forget) – is archaic and reminiscent of Morris's *If I Can* hanging (1856–57). However, chemical analysis has shown that it contains a synthetic violet dye which was not readily available until the early 1860s. Morris and his friends displayed similar hangings in the Medieval Court of the International Exhibition in 1862, which helped to establish the Firm as a viable business.

TRIAL SAMPLE FOR AN EMBROIDERED PELMET (1881–82)

Courtesy of the V&A Picture Library

Between 1880–82, the Firm carried out an extensive programme of refurbishment at St James's Palace. Among other things, this entailed the provision of new carpets and rugs, the cleaning or re-dyeing of several wall-hangings, the painting of cornices, the installation of a new chimney-piece and, finally, the production of new curtains with embroidered valances for the state rooms. This particular sample was a trial piece for the pelmets in the Blue Room and the Throne Room. The bold appliqué design, with its stylised pomegranate and swirling foliage, is outlined in couched silk braid and woven on to a length of rich damask. This features the St James's pattern – one of two new designs that were created specially for the royal commission. The overall appearance of the finished article was very regal, but the palace authorities baulked at the price, eventually persuading Morris to lower his estimate of £555 for the valances in the two chambers.

This lavish creation was far more elaborate than any of the Firm's other orders for curtains. Nonetheless, the St James's pattern remained one of their most popular (albeit expensive) lines for many years, doubtless because the conservative style of the design ensured that it never went out of fashion.

ALTAR-RAIL KNEELER (DATE UNKNOWN)

Courtesy of Christie's Images

The decoration of church interiors was always a major part of the Firm's business but, while stained-glass designs are generally well documented, textile furnishings had a much lower profile. Nevertheless, it is no accident that the main reviews of their embroideries and hangings at the 1862 International Exhibition were in publications such as *The Ecclesiologist* and *The Clerical Journal*. The production of ecclesiastical textiles remained an important aspect of the Firm's business right through to the early twentieth century, and their wares were advertised in the trade magazine, *Church Decoration*, in 1910. In the same year, they were commissioned to supply the altar hangings at Westminster Abbey for the coronation of George V.

This kneeler was produced at Merton Abbey, where Morris & Co. moved in 1881. Its simple, repeated motif is a rather weakly stylised vine-leaf and grape pattern. This is an obvious reference to the communion wine, which was placed on the altar. It could also relate to a number of Biblical passages, most notably the celebrated verses in the Gospel of St John: 'I am the vine, ye are the branches; He that abideth in me, and I in him, the same bringeth forth much fruit; for without me, ye can do nothing' (John XV:5).

PRIMROSE TILE (1862–65)

Courtesy of the V&A Picture Library

This simple, floral-pattern design is typical of the kind of tile, which Morris, Marshall, Faulkner & Co. kept amongst their stock from 1862 until the early 1870s. Its effortless stylisations are reminiscent of the embroidered hangings and curtains which were created for the Red House. Ultimately, however, the inspiration came from earlier sources; from literary sources such as illustrated flower books, or from the Dutch tradition of blue-and-white tiles which reached its zenith in the seventeenth century.

During the peak of their popularity, tiles were used in virtually any part of the home. Tile panels were placed on walls both inside and outside the house, in cellars, kitchens, dairies and fireplaces. With floral tiles, one of the most popular trends was to use them as a skirting board, so that a row of blooms appeared to be growing out of the floor. The flowers were generally stylised, with a few casual lines drawn to represent a patch of earth or a passing cloud. Even so, they were usually based on the copper engravings found in illustrated flower books. The most popular of these was the *Hortus Floridus* (1614) by Crispin de Passe.

BOUGH TILE (*c.* 1870)

Courtesy of the V&A Picture Library

Morris and his friends became interested in the artistic potential of hand-painted tiles in 1862, when they were involved in the refurbishment of the Red House. At one point, they wanted to decorate a fire-surround with tiles, but were appalled by the quality of the mass-produced items available in Britain. Undismayed, Morris imported blank tiles from Holland, which the group decorated themselves. Most of their early designs were either imitations of medieval patterns or illustrated tiles, such as the *Sleeping Beauty* series. The quartered design shown here evolved from the borders of these picture tiles. Indeed, there is a marked resemblance between the Bough pattern and part of the *Sleeping Beauty* border.

By the late 1860s, the Firm was producing far fewer picture tiles, concentrating on simple floral designs. Even in this area, there was an increasing tendency to buy in finished tiles from William de Morgan. The reason was pure economics: Morris's hand-crafted tiles were expensive to produce – the designs were always painted rather than printed onto the earthenware surface – and this enabled rival companies to manufacture similar items at more competitive prices. Several Dutch firms, for example, are known to have marketed copies of the Bough motif, and de Morgan also designed a variant of it, entitled the *Small Bough* pattern.

LONGDEN TILE (C. 1877)

Private Collection. Courtesy of the V&A Picture Library

This attractive tile, with its subtle blend of oak, bayleaf and sunflower motifs, is probably an example of the *Longden* design, which proved to be one of the Firm's most popular patterns. It was created by Philip Webb, who was paid 10 shillings for the design in 1870. The pattern was available in both yellow and blue, and was sold in the Firm's shop in Oxford Street. It was also marketed by Barnard, Bishop & Barnard, who made it up into tile panels and used them as decorative inlays in their cast-iron fireplace surrounds.

As usual, the tiles themselves were earthenware blanks, which were specially imported from Holland. These had already been glazed and fired, but their surfaces were plain and white. Morris's designs were then painted by hand on to the tiles, much of this work being carried out by Kate and Lucy Faulkner, the sisters of one of the partners in the Firm. Finally, the decorated tiles were fired for a second time in the kiln in the basement of Red Lion Square – the same kiln that was also used for their stained glass.

DAISY WALLPAPER (1864)

Courtesy of the V&A Picture Library

This was one of Morris's earliest designs, as well as one of his most enduring. It was still among the Firm's best-selling designs 50 years after its creation. The wallpaper pattern was available with a choice of three different backgrounds – light, medium and dark – and the basic design was adapted to several other media.

Morris's initial inspiration for the design came from medieval sources. The main visual impetus came from a fifteenth-century manuscript of Froissart's *Chronicles*. From this, Morris produced an embroidery design which was worked up into a curtain by Jane and Bessie Burden in the early 1860s. This was hung in the bedroom of the Red House and later transferred to Kelmscott Manor.

A second source of inspiration can be found in another of Morris's favourite texts, Chaucer's 'Legend of Good Women'. This lengthy poem began with an allegorical dream-vision about the virtues of the daisy, which was deemed 'the emperice and flour of floures alle'. Morris made a clear reference to this prologue in his designs for the decorative hangings which were to grace the walls of the drawing room in the Red House. At the foot of the surviving panels, rows of daisies are clearly visible.

DAISY TILE (1870s)

Courtesy of the V&A Picture Library

Even a cursory examination of this tile demonstrates the close affinity that existed between Morris's tiles and those produced by his counterparts in Holland. The popular *Daisy* pattern was designed by Morris in around 1862 and was sold consistently well by Morris, Marshall, Faulkner & Co. throughout the 1870s. It is a step on in design from the earlier *Primrose Tile* (1862–65), containing a series of images instead of an individual bunch of flowers. The leaves and flowers are also executed in more detail.

The *Daisy* pattern was one of Morris's favourite motifs, and it can be found in other works of the period by the Firm. In particular, it figures in his various embroidery projects for the Red House and in one of his earliest wallpaper designs. It also reflects Morris's long-time obsession with Chaucer, who praised the daisy in his writing as the most glorious of all flowers:

> *Now have I therto this condicioun,*
> *That, of all the floures in the mede,*
> *Thanne love I most these floures white and rede,*
> *Swyche as men call dayesyes in oure toun.*

SLEEPING BEAUTY TILE PANEL (1862–65)

Courtesy of the V&A Picture Library

During the early 1860s, Morris, Marshall, Faulkner & Co. produced three celebrated tile panels based on well-known fairy tales. These were *Cinderella* (1862–63), *Sleeping Beauty* (1863) and *Beauty and the Beast* (1863). The narrative scenes were designed by Burne-Jones, while the decorative border was fashioned by Morris. The border includes a marvellous series of stylised swans. Both *Beauty* and *Cinderella* are signed by Lucy Faulkner, and it is highly probable that she was also responsible for painting this series. The panel was commissioned by Myles Birket Foster for a bedroom in his house at Witley, Surrey.

Burne-Jones was unhappy with his payment for the scheme. In his notebook, he recorded, 'to ten designs of *Sleeping Beauty* at the mean and unremunerative price of 30s each.' As he tackled the subject in a number of other paintings, he may eventually have felt that it was time well spent. In 1870–73, Burne-Jones produced three small canvases on the theme for William Graham. After this, he embarked on the four large pictures known as the *Briar Rose Series* (1884–90), which are widely regarded as amongst his finest works. They were purchased for a princely sum by Lord Faringdon and installed in his house at Buscot Park, where they can still be seen today.

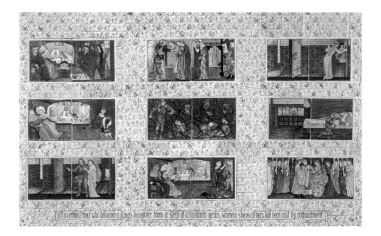

FOUR TILES (C. 1875)

Courtesy of the V&A Picture Library

Little is known about these tiles. The name of the design has not been identified and they cannot be linked with any specific commission. Nevertheless, they are typical of the work that was produced by Morris and his associates at around the time of the Membland Hall commission. Small, horizontal panels of this kind were frequently installed as overmantels; they were also used to brighten up a dull item of furniture. They can often be found adorning the top of a wooden washstand.

Morris's tile designs had developed considerably since the early days of the Firm. Initially, they reflected the widespread reawakening of interest in medieval tiles which came about as part of the Gothic revival. It is very likely that the tiles which the Firm put on show at the International Exhibition in 1862 fell into this category. By the mid-1870s, however, he was more attuned to the tastes of his well-heeled clients. Accordingly, the patterns became much closer to his textile and wallpaper designs. They take the form of leaves and tendrils, intertwining rhythmically in a foretaste of Art Nouveau.

THE KNIGHTS OF THE ROUND TABLE SUMMONED TO THE QUEST BY THE STRANGE DAMSEL (C. 1892)

Courtesy of the Birmingham Museum and Art Gallery

This is the opening scene in the *Holy Grail* series, the most important of the tapestry commissions carried out by the Firm. In 1888, Morris won an order from William Knox d'Arcy to decorate his home, Stanmore Hall, and this was his response. The daunting scheme, which consisted of five large tapestries, together with a number of smaller pieces, occupied the three looms at Merton Abbey for almost four years (1892–95).

The narrative is based on Thomas Malory's *Morte d'Arthur*. A mysterious damsel arrives unannounced in Camelot at Pentecost, and summons the knights of the Round Table to take part in the Quest. Arthur (with the crown and sceptre) and Lancelot (on the left, wearing the smaller crown) both acknowledge her challenge. At the Round Table itself, the Siege Perilous – the seat that will one day be taken by Sir Galahad – is covered in drapery bearing an inscription which prophesies that the place will soon be filled. The sacred nature of the Quest is emphasised by the presence of doves (a symbol of the Holy Ghost) above both the damsel and the Siege Perilous. The tapestry in the background bears a striking resemblance to the embroidered curtains which were produced for the bedroom at the Red House.

THE ARMING AND DEPARTURE OF THE KNIGHTS OF THE ROUND TABLE (C. 1892)

Courtesy of Birmingham Museum and Art Gallery

In this second tapestry in the *Holy Grail* series, Arthur's knights prepare to depart on their quest. The basis of the image is found in Malory's *Morte d'Arthur*, although Burne-Jones made significant alterations to the mood of the scene. In the original text, this was a melancholy occasion, with Arthur shedding a tear, realising that 'my trew felyshyp shall never mete here more agayne'. Here, the emphasis is on Lancelot, bareheaded on the left, receiving his shield from Guinevere. This is significant because it was his adulterous affair with the queen which made his heart impure and stopped him finding the Grail.

As with the other tapestries in the series, the principal elements were designed by Burne-Jones. The figures are elongated because of how the tapestry was hung at Stanmore Hall. Despite its size of 240 x 347 cm (96 x 139 in), the tapestry only covered the upper part of the dining-room wall and was meant to be seen from below. Placed beneath it was a smaller tapestry decorated with deer and coats of arms.

THE ATTAINMENT: THE VISION OF THE HOLY GRAIL (C. 1892)

Courtesy of Birmingham Museum and Art Gallery

This, the final tapestry in the *Holy Grail* series, was also destined for the dining room at Stanmore Hall. When hung there originally, its right-hand side extended over the top of a door. The tapestry was completed by 1893, when it was shown at the Arts and Crafts Exhibition.

In this scene, the questing knights have left Britain and have arrived in Sarras, the land of the Soul. Only three have been deemed worthy enough to reach their goal. Bors and Perceval are allowed to see the Grail from a distance, but three angels bar them from coming any closer. One of these holds the spear

which pierced Christ's side at the Crucifixion when, according
to the legend, Joseph of Arimathea collected His blood in the
Grail. Galahad alone progresses to the chapel where the sacred
vessel is kept, where he witnesses a vision of the Holy Ghost,
hovering above the chalice and dripping blood into it.

Burne-Jones based the Grail on an eighth-century chalice
housed in Kremsmünster Abbey in Austria. The foreground of
the tapestry features a frieze of flowers by Henry Dearle.
Burne-Jones was not happy about these, complaining that they
cluttered up his composition.

CHAIR (*C.* 1856)

Courtesy of the William Morris Gallery

Although there is no documented information relating to this chair, it seems probable that it was made and decorated by Morris, shortly after he took up residence in Red Lion Square in November 1856. His new rooms were in urgent need of new furniture, but he was unimpressed with the quality in the shops. Most commercially made furniture was designed to look good rather than to last, and as a result Morris and his friends decided to make their own chairs and tables, covering them in gaily-coloured paintings. These amateur pieces offer the first hints of their future career with the Firm.

There is little doubt that both Morris and Burne-Jones regarded this chair as a typically medieval form of design. Significantly, when the latter was planning the composition of *The Knights of the Round Table* (*c.* 1892), in the *Holy Grail* series, he included several chairs which are similar to this one. He went to the extent of engaging a carpenter to make some up, so that he could use them as 'models'. His specific source appears to have been Antonella da Messina's painting of *St Jerome in his Study*, housed in the National Gallery. After they had served their artistic purpose, these chairs were relegated to the summer house at his home in Oxfordshire, where his grandchildren were allowed to play on them.

ANGELI MINISTRANTES (1894)

Courtesy of Topham

Around 1878, Burne-Jones produced two large designs for new lancet windows in Salisbury Cathedral. Each of these drawings featured a pair of angels, who were named as *Angeli Ministrantes* and *Angeli Laudantes*. The latter carried harps with which to sing the praises of the Lord, while the Ministering Angels were dressed in the garb of pilgrims. They had shell badges on their cloaks, and carried a staff, flask and purse – all conventional symbols of pilgrims. Burne-Jones was very pleased with the results, noting in his account book, 'four colossal and sublime figures of angels £20 each'.

In later years, the same figures were adapted for use in tapestries. The general poses remained the same, but the angels were given more colourful robes; millefleurs decoration was added in the background and Henry Dearle provided a border with oranges or, as here, pomegranates. The tapestries were produced at Merton Abbey in 1894 and Morris assigned his most experienced weavers to the job. The designs were deemed particularly suitable for church use, and a number of smaller versions are in existence still. At Eton College, for example, the angel figures were adapted to form the basis of a memorial for the Boer War.

THE PROPHET SAMUEL (1868)

Courtesy of Christie's Images

This elegant stained-glass window was designed for the Firm by Burne-Jones. It depicts the Old-Testament figure of Samuel, who is shown in his traditional guise – as an old man carrying a horn. The latter refers to the passage in the Bible where the prophet took a horn of oil and anointed David as the future king of Israel (1 Samuel XVI: 13). Less traditional, however, are the trappings that surround the venerable old man. He wears a voluminous robe with a rich flower pattern, which could easily be mistaken for one of Morris's textile designs, and is set against a background of stylised leaves which are reminiscent of some of the Firm's tile panels.

Burne-Jones was already experienced in this field before the foundation of the Firm. In the late 1850s, he produced a number of designs for James Powell & Sons, most notably the St Frideswide window at Christ Church in Oxford (1859). When working for the Firm, his principal function was to prepare graceful, monochrome cartoons for individual figures. He did not include the lead-lines in his drawings, and these were added later by the glazier (Morris preferred figures that were composed of a host of tiny pieces of glass, thus creating a mosaic-like effect). By and large, Morris selected both the colour scheme and the background design of the window.

SMALL RUG WITH FLOWERPOT (1878–81)

Courtesy of Christie's Images

This is one of the small rugs Morris produced in the coach house in Hammersmith before moving this type of work to Merton Abbey. In the upper, right-hand corner of the border is the Hammersmith monogram – a hammer, a capital 'M' and stylised waves.

The pattern of the rug is close to a number of Morris's other designs from this period. These include *Lily*, which was one of his Wilton carpets, dating from 1875, and a variety of firescreens and cushion-covers. It is also particularly close to the *Flowerpot* design (*c.* 1878). Ultimately the source was a pair of seventeenth-century Italian *lacis* panels (*lacis* is a type of hand-knotted net with embroidered decoration). They were acquired in 1875 by the South Kensington Museum, where Morris would have examined them closely.

It is not known if this type of rug ever formed a regular part of the Firm's commercial stock, but they were produced in a range of colours. There is another example, in light brown and blue, kept in a collection in British Columbia, Canada. The directional axis of the pattern suggests that it was intended as a wall-hanging.

Small Rug (c. 1878–79)

Courtesy of the Castle Howard Collection

This is one of a series of small rugs that Morris produced at his Hammersmith home, Kelmscott House, in the late 1870s. Letters from the period indicate how keen he was to make progress in this field. In April 1877, he told George Wardle that he did not want to accept any new commissions 'till I get my carpets going' and, at the start of the following year, he declared: 'I want my Iceland wool tried on a rug; I will take the greatest pains in designing one when the frame [loom] is ready.'

The small rugs may well have been intended as experiments, rather than as a commercial proposition. In 1880, Morris showed his daughter that the worsted warp threads they were using on the smaller rugs were causing a problem with buckling. From that time on, the worsted was replaced with cotton.

The Howard family are known to have bought three of the small rugs and, despite any teething problems, they were impressed with their acquisitions: in February 1881, George Howard offered Morris his first major commission in this medium – a full-size carpet for the library at Naworth Castle in Cumberland.

Hammersmith Carpet (*c*. 1890)

Courtesy of Christie's Images

Morris retained happy memories of his early experiments in weaving at Kelmscott House, and the Firm's carpets were known as 'Hammersmith' carpets long after production had been transferred to Merton Abbey. This particular example was designed by Henry Dearle and dates from around 1890, when Morris started to delegate the creation of new patterns to his young associate. This transition was achieved without much difficulty, as Dearle shared Morris's fascination with Middle Eastern designs and he captured the spirit of his predecessor's work quite successfully. In general, however, his patterns were more traditional, often consisting of little more than regular, symmetrical rows of repeated motifs and patterns.

Dearle remained with the Firm for his entire career. He held two vital posts, acting as the company's art director and as the controller of the Merton Abbey works. In many ways he was effectively Morris's successor, although he became increasingly frustrated with his dual role. In particular he appears to have resented the growing influence of Henry Marillier, both in the running of the workshops and over the stylistic direction of the company's products. Nevertheless, he stayed on until his death in 1932, when his son Duncan took over as works' manager.

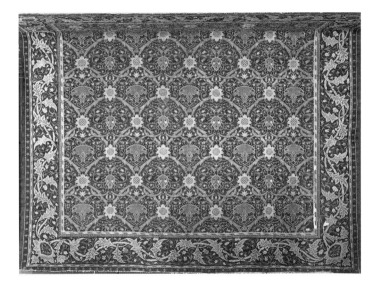

REDCAR CARPET (C. 1900s)

Courtesy of the V&A Picture Library

This design was specially created for Sir Hugh Bell in 1881. The latter lived in a Philip Webb house, Red Barns, which was situated a few miles away from Redcar itself. Red Barns had been built in 1868, but an extension was added in 1881 and Morris's carpet was intended for the drawing room in this new annexe. Bell was an important client, who had already ordered tiles, upholstery and embroidered wall-hangings from the Firm. Morris had also worked for his father, Sir Isaac Lowthian Bell, providing similar furnishings for his Yorkshire home.

The carpet was produced while Morris was operating from the coach house in Hammersmith. In February 1881, he wrote in a letter to his wife that 'Bell's carpet is well on, and I believe if it were not really dark today it would look well'. Despite his optimism, Morris was finding it hard to work in these cramped premises and was looking forward to the move to Merton Abbey, where larger looms had been installed.

The original *Redcar* carpet, which is now housed at Kelmscott Manor, has the usual Hammersmith symbol in its border. The illustrated example is a later weaving, probably dating from the early twentieth century.

DESIGN FOR REDCAR CARPET (C. 1881)

Courtesy of the V&A Picture Library

This design in pencil, watercolour and Chinese white is a preliminary sketch for the *Redcar* carpet commissioned by Sir Hugh Bell in 1881. It depicts one quarter of the proposed article on a much reduced scale (one-sixth of its eventual size). Given the symmetry of Morris's design, the sketch enabled the client to gain a clear impression of how the carpet would look when it was finished. It also gave him an opportunity to request minor changes in the pattern or the colour. Some of Morris's surviving designs carry comments, such as 'softer' or 'lighter'.

Although the design was initially drawn up for Bell's benefit, it remained a useful tool for the retailing side of the Firm. Designs of this kind could be shown to prospective clients as a form of sample book. It also enabled them to combine separate elements from different carpet designs. One of the surviving versions of the *Holland Park* carpet (1883), for example, features the ornamental border from the *Redcar* design. It is significant, too, that when Morris & Co. donated this sketch to the Victoria and Albert Museum in 1919, they reserved the right to ask for its temporary return, should it be needed for further orders.

Rug (c. 1879–81)

Courtesy of the V&A Picture Library

This rug has a close personal link with Morris's immediate circle, and was undoubtedly one of the artist's favourite designs. This particular example was given to John William Mackail and Burne-Jones's daughter, Margaret, when they were married in 1888. Mackail later went on to write the first authoritative biography of Morris, which was published in 1899. On a separate occasion, Morris also gave a copy of the rug to his sister, Henrietta.

At the time of Margaret's wedding, Morris had been established at Merton Abbey for several years. This rug was certainly made at the coach house in Hammersmith, however, for it bears the customary identifying mark in the border – the hammer, the capital 'M' and the stylised waves. It is twice as long as the smaller, experimental rugs which were also woven there, and was meant to be placed on the floor rather than the wall. This is indicated by the pattern, which can be looked at from either end, while that of the smaller rugs was meant to be viewed vertically. Morris's inspiration for this piece appears to have come from the East; the peonies and flower-heads have a distinctly Chinese flavour.

BULLERSWOOD CARPET (1889)

Courtesy of the V&A Picture Library

This is one of the most spectacular of Morris's carpet designs and also, it seems, the last in which he played a major role. The commission came from a wool merchant, John Sanderson, who was a friend of the family (Jane Morris had shared a foreign holiday with the Sandersons). It was ordered in 1889, as part of the refurbishment of Bullerswood, Sanderson's house in Chislehurst, Kent. Because of the connection between the two families, Morris appears to have supervised the project in person. In a later document (1921), it was claimed that the artist assumed full control of the drawing-room decorations, 'and nothing was allowed to be placed in it in addition to objects executed by himself, except such as met with his approval'.

The use of bird motifs shows a return to some of Morris's earliest carpet designs, but the two meandering branches, which run the full length of the piece, are much more typical of Henry Dearle's work. This has fuelled speculation that Bullerswood was a joint effort by the two men. Certainly, Morris was becoming increasingly preoccupied with his tapestry and printing projects at this time, and Dearle took over the reins of carpet production after 1890.

SAMPLE OF TULIP AND LILY (C. 1875)

Courtesy of the V&A Picture Library

Before setting up a special carpet-making division within the Firm, Morris learned his craft by working with commercial manufacturers. In the mid-1870s, he produced several designs for Kidderminster carpets, which were machine-woven by the Heckmondwike Manufacturing Company. This Yorkshire firm, which Morris referred to somewhat affectionately as 'the Heck people', had only been operating since 1873, but had already established itself as a major player in its field.

The relationship between Morris and Heckmondwike was not without its problems. At first, the preliminary process of transferring the designs on to point-paper went hopelessly awry. Morris blamed the manufacturers, claiming that their draughtsmen were incompetent, while Heckmondwike complained about the quality of his designs. Typically, Morris's solution was to train his own employees to carry out the work. The two parties also clashed over the question of plagiarism. Morris found out that Heckmondwike were producing near-identical copies of some of his more popular designs and then registering them in their own name. A *Lily and Tulip* pattern, for example, was patented by Heckmondwike in 1878. These pirated designs were then sold on to other retailers, including some of the Firm's fiercest rivals. Ultimately, problems of this kind convinced Morris that he should take full responsibility for manufacturing his own designs.

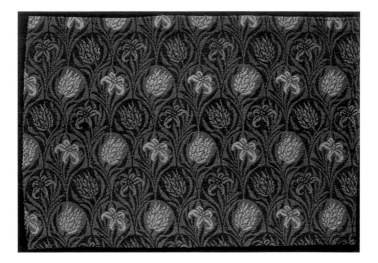

SWAN HOUSE CARPET (1881)

Courtesy of Christie's Images

This is one of two carpet designs that take their name from Swan House, situated on the Chelsea Embankment. Swan House was a Norman Shaw building which was completed in 1876, and its owner was Wickham Flower, one of Morris's most important clients. In 1881, he hired the Firm to supply many of the furnishings for the house. These included two carpets, now known as *Swan House* and *Large Swan House*, together with a range of the Firm's wallpaper and upholstery. Flower also commissioned Morris to redecorate his country retreat, Great Tangley Manor, when he moved most of his London possessions there in 1890.

The *Swan House* pattern, although very sumptuous, is generally reckoned to be one of Morris's most conservative creations. With its imposing central medallion, it is strongly reminiscent of traditional Persian carpets. Its most dramatic feature is the ornamental border – much larger than in most of Morris's other carpet designs – which encloses a running band of large palmettes. This owes its inspiration to sixteenth- and seventeenth-century Turkish models.

Copies of the *Swan House* carpet were purchased by some of Morris's other patrons. William Knox d'Arcy ordered one for the drawing room of Stanmore Hall, while another was acquired by Charles Glessner for the house that was built for him by H. H. Richardson. His version of the carpet design is now in the Art Institute of Chicago.

Detail of Peacock and Dragon Curtains (1878)

Courtesy of Christie's Images

Material of this design was used by Morris in the drawing room at Kelmscott House. He was particularly fond of *Peacock and Dragon*, believing that it came closest to his vision of the ideal medieval fabric. The entry in the Morris & Co. catalogue described it as the 'perfect hanging for a medieval castle or mansion'. This comment was more serious than one might imagine. The repeat pattern of *Peacock and Dragon* was extremely large – 107.5 x 87.5 cms, 43 x 35 ins – which meant that a wide expanse of the material was necessary if the viewer was to see it to its best advantage. At a price of 25 shillings per yard, this excluded all but the wealthiest customers.

Although Morris felt that this design was very English in spirit, its principal inspiration came from the Near and Far East. The dragons resemble the phoenixes found on Chinese textiles.

The example illustrated here shows part of a curtain, but Morris actually visualised the material as a fixed wall-covering, stretching from the ceiling to the dado. The design was available in a variety of colours, and proved extremely popular. Among the purchasers were Charles Glessner of Chicago and the Hon. Percy Wyndham, who used it at Clouds, his Wiltshire home.

BIRD CURTAINS (1877–78)

Courtesy of the V&A Picture Library

By the spring of 1877, Morris was fired with the ambition of weaving his own textiles. In a typically entrepreneurial move, he offered a one-year contract to a weaver from Lyons – brocade-weaving was still regarded as a French speciality – and installed him at Queen Square. The Frenchman, Louis Bazin, brought his own jacquard loom with him and, after a few teething problems, the operation was running smoothly by the autumn. By then, Morris had already begun to devise new patterns. He wrote to a colleague: 'I am studying birds now to see if I can't get some of them into my next design.' In the event, four of his first six designs featured birds. These were *Peacock and Dragon*, *Bird and Vine*, *Dove and Rose* and *Bird*.

Bird was the first of these designs to be completed, perhaps because Morris was already planning to use it in the drawing room of Kelmscott House, to which he moved in April 1878. Morris swathed the entire room in the fabric – all 44 feet of it – much to his family's approval. His daughter, May, described it as 'intimate and friendly ... it suggests not the wealth of the millionaire but the modest competence of a middle-class merchant who lives ... with the few beautiful things he has collected slowly and carefully'.

DOVE AND ROSE (1879)

Courtesy of the V&A Picture Library

Even after he had started composing his own designs for woven textiles, Morris was content to farm out some of the production work to outside contractors, particularly if they possessed specialist skills; *Dove and Rose* was one of these. The design involved the use of a heavy double cloth consisting of separate warps of wool and silk, which complicated the weaving process. By varying the threads which came to the surface, the weaver could create an eye-catching array of effects and textures: sometimes there were raised patterns of silk, sometimes of wool and sometimes of both.

Morris sent the *Dove and Rose* pattern to Scotland to be woven by Alexander Morton & Co. Morton had been in business since 1862, and had revived the weaving industry in Ayrshire. Although most of his employees were outworkers, the standard was high and Morris was pleased with the results. His only reservations were about the quality of the colours, which were not always fast. When discussing the durability of the fabric, he remarked to one client, 'It will last as long as need be since the cloth is really very strong. I can't answer so decidedly as to the colour...'

ANGEL OF THE RESURRECTION (1862)

Courtesy of the Tate Gallery

In the early days of the Firm, many of Morris's most important commissions came from the Church. One of their principal clients was G. F. Bodley (1827–1927), one of the leading exponents of Victorian Gothic architecture. Morris and his friends knew Bodley from the Hogarth Club, which Ford Madox Brown had founded in 1859, as a meeting point for artists and potential patrons, and he invited them to decorate three of his churches. These were St Martin-on-the-Hill in Scarborough; All Saints in Selsley and St Michael and All Angels in Brighton.

Bodley completed his work at St Michael's in 1862, when the stained glass was added by Morris, Marshall, Faulkner & Co. The highlight of the scheme was Burne-Jones's *Flight into Egypt*, and Peter Paul Marshall provided a dramatic version of *St Michael and the Dragon*. Morris's own contribution was a pair of windows in the south aisle, depicting *The Three Maries at the Sepulchre*. This is a cartoon for the left-hand section, which shows the empty tomb of Christ and the welcoming figure of the Angel of the Resurrection. Typically for Morris – and appropriately, given the style of the church – the carvings on Christ's sepulchre display a pronounced Gothic character.

ROOF DECORATION (1865)

Courtesy of the William Morris Gallery

The early decorative work carried out by Morris, Marshall, Faulkner & Co. is usually associated with newly built Gothic Revival churches, but the Firm was also involved in the restoration of some earlier churches. The most impressive example of this can be found at the Northamptonshire church of All Saints, in Middleton Cheney. The church dates mainly from the fourteenth century, but the Firm were employed there in 1865, participating in Gilbert Scott's renovations.

Middleton Cheney is justly celebrated for its windows, which may rank as the Firm's greatest achievement. There were contributions from Burne-Jones, Madox Brown, Simeon Solomon and Morris himself. The latter's designs included an unusual depiction of Eve and the Virgin Mary, together with portrayals of St Augustine, St Catherine, St Alban and St Agnes.

Because of the spectacular nature of the stained glass, the remainder of the decoration is often overlooked. In fact, the Firm repainted much of the roof in the nave and chancel. This preliminary study by Morris was for a section of one of the king-posts. It features a stylised pomegranate, a motif that he had recently used in one of his earliest wallpaper designs.

St Peter (1865)

Photo: Martyn O'Kelly. Courtesy of St Nicholas's Church, Beaudesert, Henley-in-Arden

In 1865, Thomas Garner undertook the restoration of this Warwickshire church, and Morris, Marshall, Faulkner & Co. were called in to provide several new stained-glass windows. Garner (1839–1906) was very much in the Firm's circle. He had worked in Gilbert Scott's office until 1861, and later formed a partnership with G. F. Bodley.

This figure of St Peter, designed by Morris himself, was for one of a pair of windows in the south nave. The artist's portrayal of the saint is very conventional; he holds his traditional attribute, a golden key – this refers to the passage in St Matthew: 'I will give you the keys of the kingdom of Heaven' (Matthew, XVI:19). The saint displays the key invitingly to the worshipper, while the second key – the one which opens the gates of Hell – dangles at his waist. He stands on a patch of ground which resembles Morris's *Daisy* pattern.

Philip Webb designed the pattern of diagonal bands in the background, which are decorated with stylised foliage and the saint's name. Within the church, members of the Firm produced stained-glass depictions of the Virgin, St Nicholas, St Michael and St George.

St Paul (1865)

*Photo: Martyn O'Kelly. Courtesy of St. Nicholas's Church, Beaudesert,
Henley-in-Arden*

This depiction of St Paul was one of a series of windows commissioned from the Firm by Thomas Garner during his restoration work at St Nicholas's. It formed the right-hand side of a pair of windows in the south nave, facing Morris's version of St Peter. The figure was designed by Ford Madox Brown, who was closely involved in many of the Firm's commissions. Brown (1821–93) was an elder statesman of the Pre-Raphaelite movement and a founding member of the Firm. He remained with the company, designing stained glass and furniture, until Morris reorganised the business in 1875.

St Paul is shown with two of his traditional attributes, a scroll and a sword. The former is a reference to his role as the author of the Epistles, while the sword relates to his execution. The latter is particularly common in scenes where Peter and Paul are represented together since, according to tradition, they were martyred in Rome on the same day. Peter was crucified while Paul, as a Roman citizen, was granted the privilege of being executed by the sword. In stained-glass schemes, the two saints were often portrayed together because they were regarded as the joint founders of the Christian Church; Peter represented the earlier Jewish element and Paul the gentiles.

TAPESTRY OF THE ANNUNCIATION (1911)

Courtesy of Christie's Images

The Firm flourished for more than 40 years following Morris's death in 1896. It was initially acquired by his junior partners, Frank and Robert Smith, who remained in sole charge until 1905, when four new directors were appointed and the firm was renamed Morris & Co. Decorators Ltd.

One of the newcomers was Henry Currie Marillier, who remained with the company until its closure in 1940. He is mainly remembered today as Morris's first biographer, but he had an abiding interest in historic tapestries, producing studies on the tapestry collection at Hampton Court (1931) and Teniers (1932). Marillier was largely responsible for the tapestries produced at Merton Abbey. With the death of Burne-Jones in 1898, the Firm lost its chief designer in this field, and its later output consisted mainly of copies of paintings or stained-glass windows. Given that most of the commissions for tapestries came from churches, there was a shift away from Arthurian and purely decorative themes towards scenes from the Scriptures. This example is a copy of an *Annunciation* painted by Fra Filippo Lippi (*c.* 1406–69). It brought the work of the Firm full-circle, for it was the work of early Italian artists that had inspired the original Pre-Raphaelite movement.

MINSTREL (C. 1874)

Courtesy of the V&A Picture Library

Although Morris's approach to many aspects of his art was idealistic, he also had strong commercial instincts. This is most evident from the way that he sought to maximise the potential of his most popular designs. Certain images and themes – for instance, the *Daisy* pattern or the 'Legend of Good Women' – recur again and again in his work, adapted to a variety of different media.

The *Minstrel* designs offer a case in point. Morris created a series of 12 figures with musical instruments, employing them in a number of stained-glass, tile and tapestry commissions. The idea was particularly suitable for stained-glass panels, which could be used to decorate either a private home or a church, for, with the addition of a pair of wings, the minstrel could easily be transformed into an angel.

This is one of the secular minstrels. In addition to the lack of wings, the figure is set against a background of Morris's favourite floral motifs. The alternating panels depict stylised sunflowers and daisies, both of which featured regularly in his textile designs. He used this particular backdrop on many of his secular commissions since the panels were usually ordered in pairs and this helped to unify the different figure styles.

WOMAN PLAYING LUTE (C. 1874)

Courtesy of the V&A Picture Library

The series of 12 figures in this format showed minstrels as either secular or angelic musicians, depending on their context. This particular illustration shows one of the minstrels, set against a background of sunflowers and daisies. This panel may have been made around 1874, but the figure had already been used in a number of church commissions by that date. In 1869, for example, Morris had included a near-identical figure in his decorative scheme at Tilehurst church. The chief differences between the two are that the Tilehurst angel possessed a pair of crimson wings and was set against quarries (background panels) of a deep blue firmament with starry spirals. The same group also included an angel with cymbals, which was very similar to the Dalton figure pictured below.

Morris's inspiration for his *Minstrel* series undoubtedly came from medieval sources. Musicians were frequently portrayed on misericords or in illuminated manuscripts. They were also especially common in psalters (manuscripts of the *Book of Psalms*), most notably the *Luttrell Psalter* in the British Museum. Morris's portrayal of the musical instruments was deliberately archaic and occasionally eccentric. Here, for example, the tapering shape of the instrument and the way it is held suggest that it is a rebec (a bowed instrument), whereas the strumming action indicates a lute.

MINSTREL WITH CYMBALS (C. 1868)

Courtesy of Christie's Images

This angelic musician was designed by Morris as part of the decorations at St John's Church in Dalton, near York. It bears a close resemblance to the *Minstrel* series, which was adapted for use in private homes. Examples of *Minstrels with Cymbals* can be found at Wightwick Manor in Wolverhampton and at the Ashmolean Museum.

Unlike most of Morris's other angelic musicians, the Dalton figure has no wings. In this, it differs from the more elegant versions at Tilehurst and Lewknor. This may well have something to do with the dimensions of the Dalton window, which is both shorter and broader than those at the other locations. While the minstrels were purely decorative, the angels' function was to adore. In the Tilehurst window, for instance, the five musicians are placed around figures of the Virgin and Child, singing their praises. Morris's inspiration for this may have come from a painting such as Piero della Francesca's *Nativity* at the National Gallery in London, which depicts an angelic orchestra celebrating the arrival of the newborn Christ.

Morris's angels were also notable for their fine flesh tints, which were achieved by the use of enamel paint. 'Finding that it was difficult to get flesh-coloured glass with tone enough for the flesh,' Morris explained, 'we used thin washes of reddish enamel colour to stain white glass.'

CHAIR (C. 1857)

Courtesy of Christie's Images

This high-backed chair, which is one of a pair, is typical of the flamboyant furniture that Morris and his friends produced, during their days at Red Lion Square. Burne-Jones and Morris moved into their new lodgings at the end of 1856 and, almost immediately, began to decorate it in their own inimitable manner. Wishing to create a medieval oasis in the heart of the modern metropolis, they employed a local cabinet-maker to produce some suitable items of furniture. They then proceeded to decorate these with bright patterns and vivid pictures, hoping to capture the spirit of the images seen in early manuscripts and tapestries. Rossetti, who was a regular visitor, offered to join in the fun and help them.

The painting on this chair is thought to be one of Rossetti's contributions. The theme has been identified as *The Arming of a Knight*, which accords very well with his subject matter of the period. A nobleman kneels before his lady, who pins her favour to his hat. This is comparable with his watercolour *Before the Battle*, where a lady attaches a pennant to her lover's spear. Rossetti painted this in 1857, borrowing the subject from Lizzie Siddal, who had tackled a similar subject in the previous year.

TOPSY AND NED JONES SETTLED ON THE SETTLE IN RED LION SQUARE (C. 1922)

Courtesy of the Tate Gallery, London

With his plump figure and shock of hair, Morris was always a tempting subject for caricaturists. Throughout his life, he was known as 'Topsy', a name borrowed from a character in *Uncle Tom's Cabin*, while Edward Burne-Jones was called 'Ned'. Both Rossetti and Burne-Jones produced numerous caricatures of Morris. These frequently portrayed him reading, as he was notorious for regaling his friends with his own writings, reciting them in monotonous, droning tones. Georgiana Burne-Jones remembered '...often falling asleep to the steady rhythm of the reading voice, or biting my fingers and stabbing myself with pins in order to keep awake'.

Max Beerbohm's satirical watercolour dates from a later age, when the Pre-Raphaelites were deeply unfashionable. It was made for an entire volume of caricatures on Rossetti and his circle, in which Morris was characterised as something of a ranter (he was as well known for his political views, as for his art), and Burne-Jones was portrayed as a lanky aesthete. In some senses, Beerbohm was still building on the public image of artists which had been formed in Gilbert and Sullivan's *Patience* (1881). This portrayed painters as effete dreamers – a view which seems to be reinforced by the languid figure shown on the settle underneath Morris's legs.

Painted Panel (C. 1857)

Courtesy of the V&A Picture Library

This is one of a group of four oil panels which are currently housed at the Victoria and Albert Museum. Their attribution has been the subject of much debate. Two of the panels – those portraying the girl on the ladder and the girl drinking from a fountain – were donated to the museum in 1960. The gift came from Christabel Marillier, who was the wife of Rossetti's first biographer. She indicated that the scenes were by Rossetti. The remaining two pictures were acquired from a market in Romford in 1953, when it was suggested that the artist was Morris. To complicate matters still further, some authorities have rejected both these attributions and assigned the paintings to Burne-Jones. They have done so largely on stylistic grounds, citing a resemblance to the figures in his *Ladies and Animals Sideboard* (date about 1860) and to his painting of *Fair Rosamund*.

In fact, without the benefit of documented evidence, it is impossible to make an attribution with any confidence. However, the paintings date from a formative period in the lives of the three artists when they were in frequent contact and influencing each other considerably.

PAINTED PANEL (C. 1857)

Courtesy of the V&A Picture Library

The subject of the four painted panels now owned by the Victoria and Albert Museum has given rise to as much debate as the question of attribution. One of the most popular views is that they represent the four seasons. This has been a commonplace theme for artists over the centuries and, of course, it traditionally consists of four scenes. Nevertheless, it raises a number of problems. Two of the pictures – the girl climbing up a ladder to smell a sprig of blossom, and the woman bending down to look at a nest in a blossoming shrub – appear to represent springtime subjects, while the image of the girl at a fountain does not contain obvious seasonal implications. There is no reason to suppose that the pictures were designed as a set of four. There may have been other scenes, now lost, or they may have been intended as two pairs of panels.

It is likely that the scenes were meant to be purely decorative, although there are overtones of the *hortus conclusus* (enclosed garden), a popular medieval theme which Morris and his friends would have known from manuscripts. It was most closely associated with Mary and implied both virginity and fecundity (symbolised in the fruit, the blossoms and the fountain).

Painted Panel (c. 1857)

Courtesy of the V&A Picture Library

One of the likeliest explanations for this group of four panel paintings is that they were designed to be set into an item of furniture. The illustrated side of the *St George Cabinet* and the panelled settle portrayed in Max Beerbohm's caricature of *Topsy and Ned Jones* (*c.* 1922) both give an indication of how the pictures might have been used. It is true that the scenes on the *St George* cabinet and on several similar pieces (such as *King René's Honeymoon* cabinet and *The Prioress's Tale* wardrobe) contain specific narrative elements, but this was not always the case. Morris and his friends also worked on items that were purely decorative, such as *The Backgammon Players* cabinet and the *Ladies and Animals* sideboard.

In most cases, the group did not actually make the furniture themselves. They employed a local cabinet maker named Henry Price to produce the pieces to their specifications, and then added their own painted decoration. In his diary, Price mentioned how he was asked to build old-fashioned furniture in the medieval style, specifying this more precisely as 'tables and high-backed chairs, like what I have seen in Abyes and Cathedrals'.

PAINTED PANEL (C. 1857)

Courtesy of the V&A Picture Library

This is the most Rossettian of the figures in the four painted panels which were produced in the late 1850s. Rossetti was particularly fond of portraying some of his female figures in this distinctive horned cap, a variation of the so-called 'butterfly' headdress. In *The Arming of a Knight*, for example, it is worn by two of the women in the background, and it features even more prominently in such paintings as *Sir Galahad* and *The Tune of Seven Towers*.

Whoever the artist may have been, the panels were surely meant to adorn one of the striking pieces of furniture in Red Lion Square. All three artists participated keenly in their creation, as a comment from Burne-Jones confirms: 'Topsy has had some furniture (chairs and table) made after his own design; they are as beautiful as mediaeval work, and when we have painted designs of knights and ladies upon them they will be perfect marvels.' Burne-Jones's enthusiasm for these pieces was shared by the many visitors to Red Lion Square. When a meeting of the Hogarth Club was held there, for example, one member eulogised the 'drawings, tapestries and furniture, the latter gorgeously painted in subjects by Jones and Morris and Gabriel Rossetti'.

Preliminary Drawing for the St George Cabinet (1861)

Courtesy of the V&A Picture Library

This is Morris's preliminary sketch for the first panel of his *St George Cabinet*. The demands of the narrative persuaded him to partition the side of the chest into a number of unequal segments, a clumsy device which mars the overall balance of the composition.

Little is known about the real St George, but Morris based his pictures on one of the medieval versions of the story. His likeliest source would have been the *Golden Legend*, a compendium of saints' lives, myths and commentaries which had been published by Caxton in 1483. Morris was very fond of this book, eventually acquiring more than 10 different editions of it, and he planned to make it the opening publication of the Kelmscott Press.

The medieval version of the legend places the action at Silene in Libya. There, the townsfolk were being terrorised by a fierce dragon. In order to pacify the beast, young maidens were offered up to it at regular intervals. These victims were chosen by lot and, after a time, the king's daughter, Princess Sabra, drew the unlucky token. This is the episode shown here. The princess is led off by soldiers, while the king looks away in despair.

PRELIMINARY DRAWING FOR THE
ST GEORGE CABINET (1861)

Courtesy of the V&A Picture Library

This is Morris's study for the left-hand portion of the central panel. The princess has been tied to a pole and left to await the arrival of the dragon. In the finished version of the panel, there was a note affixed to the pole, explaining the maiden's fate. In most versions of the story, both in literature and in art, this episode took place on an island or by the seashore, but Morris chose to set the scene at the edge of a dense wood. The model for the princess was his wife, Jane.

The subject of St George was a popular one among artists, and Morris had doubtless studied many other depictions of the theme. There were versions by Tintoretto and Uccello in London's National Gallery, and he may well have seen reproductions of Carpaccio's famous murals. It is likely, however, that some of his enthusiasm for the subject came from Rossetti, who had already produced a beguiling watercolour of *The Wedding of St George and the Princess Sabra* (1857). The details of the story are also very close to the myth of Perseus and Andromeda, which had been portrayed countless times by earlier artists. Indeed, some versions of the St George legend located it in Beirut, where Perseus's feat had also taken place.

PRELIMINARY DRAWING FOR THE ST GEORGE CABINET (1861)

Courtesy of the V&A Picture Library

This drawing relates to the key incident in the St George legend. The hero has just slain the dragon, which lies dead on the ground beside him, and he now turns to release Princess Sabra from her bonds. In the completed picture, Morris added the sword, which is lodged firmly in the dragon's gullet.

The composition of the scene is closely related to Rossetti's *St George and the Princess Sabra*. The poses of the central characters are very similar, and it seems highly likely that one artist influenced the other. Which came first is hard to tell, since both artists began illustrating the subject at around the same time. The Rossetti picture has an added poignancy, however, since the model was Lizzie Siddal, the princess he was unable to save. She was already ill and died in February 1862.

The weakest section of Morris's sketch is the dragon, which one critic likened to 'a stuffed crocodile'. The artist later rectified this, managing to produce a much more fearsome creature when he was working in fabric. His *Peacock and Dragon* design, which dates from 1878, was a far superior creation.

PRELIMINARY DRAWING FOR THE ST GEORGE CABINET (1861)

Courtesy of the V&A Picture Library

This is the final drawing in the St George narrative, which filled the entire right-hand panel of the cabinet. In this, the hero leads Princess Sabra in a triumphant procession back to town, where he will claim her as his bride. This serves as a pretext for a colourful scene of medieval pageantry, very much in the spirit of the painted furniture from Red Lion Square or pictures such as *Sir Degrevaunt's Wedding Feast*.

In both the sketches and the completed paintings on the cabinet, Morris stripped the St George legend of its religious content, visualising it instead as a romantic fairy-tale. In this, he went further than either Rossetti or Burne-Jones, both of whom retained some Christian elements, however cursory, in their treatment of the theme. He also departed from his medieval sources, which used the heroic deed as a parable of Christian faith. In the legend, St George only agrees to slay the dragon (a conventional symbol of paganism) and rescue the maiden (the personification of the area), if the townspeople will agree to convert to Christianity. Accordingly, the final scene is not so much a celebration of a single marriage as a rejoicing in the salvation of the collective soul of the entire community.

St George Cabinet (1861)

Courtesy of the V&A Picture Library

This is one of the most elaborate pieces of furniture that Morris and his friends produced during their time in the Red House. The cabinet itself was designed by Philip Webb and made from mahogany, oak and pine. The surface was then gilded and decorated with scenes from the legend of St George, by Morris himself. Only one side of the cabinet was painted, as it was designed to stand against a wall. The interior was painted in a shade of red, which was 'as rich as dragon's blood'.

In many ways, this cabinet marks the coming of age of the Firm. It displays the same exuberance as much of the furniture produced in Red Lion Square, but it also managed to dispel many of the amateurish qualities which had marred some of the Firm's early pieces. It was completed early in 1862, in time to be shown at the International Exhibition of Art and Industry. There, the cabinet formed the centrepiece of one of their stands, adorned with glassware created by Philip Webb. It was priced at 50 guineas but, despite a fairly enthusiastic reception, failed to sell.

Ceiling Design (c. 1880)

Courtesy of the William Morris Society

Some of Morris's wealthier clients went far beyond the purchase of a single pair of curtains or a new set of upholstery, and hired the Firm to refurbish entire rooms. This watercolour sketch of a floral design for the drawing-room ceiling relates to one of the Firm's most elaborate commissions, the decoration of A. A. Ionides' London house at 1 Holland Park. The sketch was executed by either Webb or Morris, and the estimate for the ceiling amounted to £160.

The work at Ionides' house was carried out in three stages between 1880 and 1888. In the drawing room, the floral effect on the ceiling was echoed in the specially designed *Holland Park* carpet (1883), precursor to the later *Hammersmith* carpet (*c.* 1890), and on the grand piano, also provided by Morris & Company. On this, Kate Faulkner executed a delicate network of flowers. Elsewhere in the house, a wide variety of Morris's fabrics were in evidence, including *Flower Garden*, *Oak*, *Bird* and *Utrecht Velvet*. Ionides, who had made his fortune as a cotton importer and financier, also purchased *The Forest* tapestry, which hung in his study.

No 1 Holland Park (Ionides)
Drawing Room Ceiling

SELF-PORTRAIT (1856)

Courtesy of the V&A Picture Library

This capable self-portrait, dated July 29th, shows Morris as a young man, on the threshold of his artistic career. As a student, he had seemed destined for a life in the Church, but a tour of the cathedrals of northern France in the company of Burne-Jones made him think again. Both men vowed to dedicate themselves to art: Burne-Jones as a painter and Morris as an architect. With this in mind, Morris signed articles with George Street, one of the leading architects of the Gothic Revival, and began his training in January 1856. This picture was made during his brief spell with Street. He is even shown wearing his working smock.

Morris stayed with Street for less than a year, but the latter's influence was invaluable. Beside his passion for all things Gothic – his best-known buildings are the Law Courts in London – Street's knowledge ranged over a wide area, including stained-glass design, wrought-ironwork and textiles. Morris soon began to share some of these interests, but he found the daily routine of office work utterly demoralising. Compared with this, Burne-Jones's way of life, working as a pupil under Rossetti, seemed increasingly tempting. So, in November 1856, Morris left Street's practice and moved into Red Lion Square.

JANE BURDEN (1857)

Courtesy of the British Museum

In the summer of 1857, Rossetti persuaded a group of friends, Morris among them, to help him paint a series of murals in the Oxford Union. With a spirit of adventure, the companions set to work, casting around for local girls who might model for them. One of these was Jane Burden, the 17-year-old daughter of an ostler. Rossetti met her in a temporary theatre in the old Music Room and badgered her into posing for him and his friends. All were smitten by her beauty. As Rossetti's brother, William, remarked, 'her face was at once tragic, mystic, passionate, calm, beautiful and gracious – a face for a sculptor, and a face for a painter – a face solitary in England.'

Jane was spellbound by the charm of Rossetti, but he was still involved with Lizzie Siddal. Instead, it was his disciple, Morris, who pressed his suit. By the time he drew this portrait, in late September, Morris was already in love with her. It is tempting to believe that he may even have had the picture in front of him when he composed 'Praise of My Lady', his first love poem for Jane.

Iseult Boarding the Ship (c. 1857)

Courtesy of the William Morris Gallery

This is one of Morris's earliest drawings, dating from the time when he was still hoping to forge a career as a painter. It may have been executed while he was still in Oxford, working on the Union murals. His inexperience shows through in his faulty technique: the head is finely drawn, as are the patterns on the sleeve, but the articulation of the body and the hands – in particular the position of the left hand – is weak.

Morris was much preoccupied with the theme of Tristram and Iseult at this time. The somewhat ponderous theme of his mural at the Union was *How Sir Palomydes loved la Belle Iseult with Exceeding Great Love* and he followed this up with *La Belle Iseult*. Apart from these, the titles of two other proposed paintings are known: *Tristram recognised by Iseult's Dog* and *Tristram and Iseult on the Ship*. Neither of these appear to have been completed, although this drawing of Jane was presumably a study for the latter. In all probability, the agonies which he suffered when trying to paint *La Belle Iseult* eventually persuaded him that his talents would be better employed in other fields.

THE FOREST TAPESTRY (1887)

Courtesy of the V&A Picture Library

One of Morris's greatest strengths was his skill in co-ordinating the talents of his many different associates. By common assent, *The Forest* is among the finest of the collaborative works produced by Morris & Company. The birds and animals were designed by Philip Webb, based on a charming series of drawings. Morris incorporated these into a background of swirling acanthus which evokes memories of the *Acanthus and Vine* (*c.* 1879) tapestry, his first venture in this field. In the foreground, floral details were added by Henry Dearle, who performed a similar function in the *Holy Grail* series (*c.* 1892). Finally, an

embroidered inscription was blazoned across the centre of the tapestry: 'The beasts that be in woodland waste, now sit and see nor ride nor haste'. Morris expanded on the theme in 'The Lion', which was published in his *Poems by the Way* (1891).

The Forest was woven at Merton Abbey by three of Morris's most experienced operatives: William Knight, John Martin and William Sleath. The tapestry was shown at the 1890 Arts and Crafts Exhibition and was purchased by A. A. Ionides. He hung it in the study of his house at 1 Holland Park, alongside a smaller Morris tapestry of acanthus leaves.

DESIGN FOR ACANTHUS AND PEACOCKS (1879–81)

Courtesy of the V&A Picture Library

This subtle watercolour design probably dates from the late 1870s, when Morris was conducting his earliest experiments in tapestry-making. It has close affinities with *Acanthus and Vine*, his first completed tapestry, and may even predate it. There is a theory that he abandoned the design because it was too difficult for him to attempt while still a novice at the art. Certainly it is easy to see the attraction of the theme. Morris loved to create visual ambiguities with his intricate, swirling patterns and it takes a moment for the viewer to separate the sweep of the peacocks' tails from the curving fronds of acanthus and palm. This was a device which Morris had already perfected in his wallpapers and his textiles.

Morris launched into tapestry making with his customary enthusiasm and energy. He installed a traditional high-warp loom in his bedroom at Kelmscott House and practised on it diligently in spare moments. He was scathing about modern, commercial tapestries, most of which were copies of oil paintings, and called for a return to the standards of the Flemish weavers in the Middle Ages. 'Tapestry is a bright dream,' he told one of his colleagues, adding in a later lecture that it was 'the noblest of the weaving arts, in which there is nothing mechanical'.

CARTOON FOR ACANTHUS AND VINE (1879)

Courtesy of the V&A Picture Library

In later life, Morris always claimed that it was the glories of early tapestries that first turned his attention towards art. One of his most vivid boyhood memories was of a visit to Queen Elizabeth's Hunting Lodge in Epping Forest, where he was greatly impressed by 'a room hung with faded greenery'. This early interest was reinforced in the mid-1850s when he went on a tour of French cathedrals with Burne-Jones.

Morris did not have a chance to recapture the magic of those early memories until the late 1870s, when he took the decision to add tapestry-making to the Firm's repertoire. This cartoon, executed in pencil and watercolour, is a full-size, working study for his first completed tapestry. In it, Morris strove to emulate the 'faded greenery' that he had witnessed as a child, deliberately using a range of muted colours. The official title of the tapestry was *Acanthus and Vine* but, due to the tightly coiled appearance of the acanthus leaves, it was rapidly dubbed *Cabbage and Vine* by the Morris household. Morris wove the tapestry in his bedroom at Kelmscott House, taking a phenomenal 516 hours to complete it.

DESIGN FOR ARTICHOKE HANGING (1877)

Courtesy of Topham

Morris was not only commissioned to produce complete artworks for his clients. Occasionally, he was asked to create designs which gifted people could then make for themselves. This particular design was ordered by Mrs Ada Godman, the daughter of Isaac Lowthian Bell, one of Morris's most important customers. With it, she created an ambitious scheme of wall hangings at Smeaton Manor in Northallerton, a house designed for the family by Philip Webb. These embroidered panels were originally intended for the drawing room alone, but Mrs Godman later extended the decoration, reproducing the design in a number of different colour combinations. She was apparently still adding to the scheme in 1900.

Designs of this kind did not become the exclusive property of the client, and Morris is known to have sold the *Artichoke* pattern to a number of other customers. Most notable of these was Mrs Margaret Beale, a highly talented needlewoman. Together with her daughters, she produced a version of the *Artichoke* hanging, highlighted in silk. This is displayed in the North Bedroom at Standen, their home in West Sussex which is now owned by the National Trust.

LOTUS HANGING (1875–80)

Courtesy of the V&A Picture Library

This is one of Morris's earliest designs for a hanging, dating from the late 1870s. The pattern is built up from simple, repeated motifs. Although, unlike block-printed or woven textiles, embroidery did not require repetitions of this kind, it was the format that Morris preferred at this time. In later designs, he switched to quartered, mirror-image patterns. The hanging itself was not manufactured by the Firm, but was produced by the client, Mrs Margaret Beale. Working in silk, she executed the design in delicate shades of peach and brown. She was obviously pleased with the results, for in about 1896, she and her daughters embroidered a hanging in the *Artichoke* design.

The Beales were enthusiastic clients of Morris. James Beale was a solicitor working for the railways, and Margaret was an expert needlewoman, involved in the foundation of the Royal School of Art Needlework (1872). It is no accident that her portrait by William Nicholson shows her knitting. The Beales lived at 32 Holland Park in London, and were probably introduced to Morris through their neighbours, the Ionides family. In 1894, the Beales moved to Standen. The house was designed by Philip Webb and the family furnished it with many of the Firm's products.

OAK DESIGN (1881)

Courtesy of the V&A Picture Library

This sumptuous silk damask was one of the most luxurious and expensive of the Firm's fabrics. It was designed by Morris in 1880–81, after he received a second commission for decorations at St James's Palace (the Firm had refurbished the Tapestry Room and Armoury in 1866–67). On this occasion, the authorities wanted to redecorate the Blue Room and the Throne Room. Morris offered them two new designs, *St James's* and *Oak*, which met with official approval. The commission proved a lucrative one; an estimate for the *Oak* curtains in the Throne Room amounted to £750, and the total bill for the work in the Palace – including a great deal of cleaning, restoration and re-upholstering – came to over £10,000.

By Morris's standards, the *Oak* pattern was extremely conventional. In spite of this, it proved very popular with the Firm's clients, and remained on the books long after Morris's death. A catalogue dated around 1910 shows that it was available in six shades of figured silk at 45 shillings per yard, and in five shades of damask at 33 shillings 6 pence per yard. The design was revived briefly in the 1950s by Sandersons, when it was re-named *Whittingaeme*.

GRANADA DESIGN (1884)
Courtesy of the V&A Picture Library

Morris never ceased experimenting and this, one of his last textile designs, demonstrates that the results were not always successful. His original idea was to produce a modern version of the lush brocaded velvets which had been so popular in the fifteenth and sixteenth centuries. Unfortunately, the weaving process was complicated and it proved necessary to build a special loom at Merton Abbey for the production of this one item.

In technical terms, the new machine proved a success and the fabric was greeted with acclaim. *The Art Journal* declared that it was 'the only English velvet that bears any comparison to the old Flemish velvets'. Even so, the time and money invested in the project was never recouped. The cost of producing the *Granada* design was so prohibitive that any thoughts of commercial production were abandoned. In the end, just 20 yards were woven, selling at the incredible price of £10 per yard, the most expensive of all Morris's textiles. A six-foot length of the material remained unsold; this was exhibited in France in 1919 and then sold to the Victoria and Albert Museum for £35.

TULIP AND NET (1888–89)

Courtesy of the V&A Picture Library

By the late 1880s, Morris was increasingly being diverted away from textile design by other projects. He was more interested in tapestry making; his political activities were becoming more time-consuming; and he began to toy with the idea of founding his own private press. Accordingly, after 1888 he passed the responsibility for developing new textile lines over to John Henry Dearle.

Dearle (1860–1932) was well equipped to take over the reins. He had been with the Firm since 1878, when he was employed as a shop assistant at their Oxford Street outlet. From there, he progressed rapidly, training as a glass-painter and weaver before eventually becoming manager of the tapestry workshop at Merton Abbey. After Morris's death, he was appointed art director of the Firm. *Tulip and Net* was one of his first designs and it displays the influence of earlier Persian textiles. In general, his work was more formalised and less naturalistic than Morris's, but it was very popular and had a very long shelf-life. In Morris & Co.'s *Church Decoration and Furniture* catalogue of around 1910, *Tulip and Net* was advertised as suitable for church use.

TULIP AND ROSE (1876)

Courtesy of the V&A Picture Library

Tulip and Rose was registered on 20 January 1876, making it Morris's earliest recorded design for a woven furnishing textile. It dates from the period when the Firm were still contracting out large-scale weaving orders to commercial manufacturers. This design was produced by the Heckmondwike Manufacturing Company, the same Yorkshire firm that had handled his *Tulip and Lily* carpeting in the previous year. It has been suggested that *Tulip and Rose* may also have been designed with carpeting in mind, but it was registered specifically as a textile design and no specific examples of its use as a floor covering have been recorded.

Even so, versatility was one of the greatest virtues of the *Tulip and Rose* pattern. The pictured example, from the Victoria and Albert Museum, is a curtain made of triple-ply woollen cloth with silk trim. The same design – though in a combination of light green and red – was used at Wightwick Manor in Wolverhampton to cover a sofa and some cushions; while at Standen, the Beale family home in West Sussex, there are *Tulip and Rose* hangings made from a silk and cotton mix, in both the billiard room and the drawing room.

WOODPECKER TAPESTRY (1885)

Courtesy of Topham

This is probably Morris's most famous tapestry and one of only three which he designed entirely by himself. It features a delicate border of trailing honeysuckle and a verse inscription, which was embroidered by May Morris and her assistants.

The central panel offers a combination of two of Morris's favourite themes – nature and mythology. The lower part of the composition is dominated by the swirling acanthus leaves which dominated so many of the artist's other tapestries (most notably *The Forest* and *Acanthus and Vine*). The upper part relates to a story from Ovid's *Metamorphoses* in which Picus, the king of Ausonia, marries a beautiful nymph named Canens, who can charm the trees and the rocks with the dulcet tones of her voice. Picus is devoted to her but, while out on a hunting expedition, he crosses the path of Circe, a powerful sorceress. She offers Picus her love and, when he rejects this, she transforms him into a bird. He then flees into a wood, angrily attacking the trees with his beak in frustration at his cruel fate. He is the woodpecker referred to in the inscription as 'once a king' and now 'the tree-bark's thief'.

PRELIMINARY DESIGN (C. 1880)

Courtesy of Christie's Images

Morris's intricate flower patterns, which seem so effortless and casual in their final form, were achieved after long hours of patient draughtsmanship and the production of dozens of different designs. This preliminary stage was all-important, as Morris recognised. In a lecture called 'Making the Best of It', delivered in 1879, he offered these words of advice to potential designers: 'no amount of delicacy is too great in drawing the curves of a pattern, no amount of care in getting the leading lines right from the first, can be thrown away, for beauty of detail cannot afterwards cure any shortcomings in this.'

The pictured example comes from Morris's mature years, when his designs exhibited increasing freedom. It has some affinities with the *St James's* pattern, which Morris devised specifically for the second refurbishment programme at St James's Palace. This was carried out between 1880 and 1882 and shows why Morris was such an important influence on the Art Nouveau movement. His flower patterns have just enough naturalism and depth to be convincing, but it is the rhythm and sweep of the stylised foliage which lend them their true appeal.

DESIGN FOR TRELLIS WALLPAPER (1862)

Courtesy of the William Morris Gallery

This was Morris's first attempt at designing a wallpaper pattern but, owing to technical problems, it was only the third one to be issued. The design was not officially registered until February 1864, some 15 months after Morris completed his layout.

The trellis had long been a popular motif in wallpaper design, but Morris may have had a personal reason for choosing it. It is often suggested that he was inspired by his garden at the Red House, which featured 'wattled rose-trellises enclosing richly flowered square garden plots'. He was also particularly fond of the wild rose, declaring that 'nothing can be more beautiful than a wayside bush of it, nor can any scent be as sweet and pure as its scent'.

The birds in this watercolour study and in the completed design, are by Philip Webb. Both he and Morris retained a great affection for the pattern, and Morris used it in his own home. His daughter, May, recorded vivid memories of the wallpaper from her nursery days at Queen Square. She would lie awake at night, staring at one of the birds 'because he was thought to be wicked and very alive'.

Fruit Wallpaper (c. 1866)

Courtesy of the V&A Picture Library

This design is sometimes known as *Pomegranate*, although *Fruit* is clearly a more accurate title, since the pattern also includes lemons, oranges and peaches. There is also a degree of confusion over its date. Traditionally, it has been seen as one of the earliest Morris wallpapers, dating from 1864. However, both Mackail (Morris's first biographer) and Campfield (a foreman employed by the Firm) have confirmed that the artist was still working on the design a year or so later. This might also explain the very close resemblance between this pattern and the decorated panels in the Green Dining Room at the South Kensington Museum, executed in 1866.

Like *Daisy*, the pattern which preceded it, *Fruit* was available with a choice of three different background colours: light, medium and dark. Its composition, however, was rather more complex. The rectangular structure of the repeat pattern was masked by the pale diagonal of the branches and the subtle background of twigs and berries. In addition, while the daisies appear rigidly two-dimensional, Morris's fruits are more naturalistic. There is light stippling on their surfaces, and the burst skins and exposed seeds of the over-ripe pomegranates lend an extra hint of realism.

DESIGN FOR SUNFLOWER WALLPAPER (1877–78)

Courtesy of the William Morris Society

This is Morris's original design, executed in pen and watercolour, for one of his most schematic patterns. It dates from his second phase of wallpaper design, which lasted from approximately 1876 to 1882. During this time, Morris was growing increasingly interested in the weaving process, and some of the stylistic traits commonly associated with that craft were carried over into his wallpaper design. In particular, he started to adopt the vertical 'turnover' (or mirror-image repeat), which is characteristic of woven textiles. As a result, the fruit and flowers in *Sunflower* are more stylised than those in earlier designs, and no effort is made to disguise the strictly symmetrical appearance of the pattern. *Sunflower* was registered in January 1879, at the same time as *Acorn*, which displays similar characteristics.

The *Sunflower* paper sold well, partly because it was one of Morris's cheaper designs, selling at around five shillings per unit, and partly because the flower itself was very fashionable at the time. This may have encouraged Morris to contemplate a more sumptuous version of the design. In place of the pale yellows and blues, he printed the pattern in red oil colour on a lacquered gold background, which sold for 30 shillings a roll.

HONEYSUCKLE CURTAIN OR HANGING (1876)

Private Collection. Courtesy of the V&A Picture Library

This was May Morris's favourite design. She described it as 'the most truly Morrisian in character of all his pattern-making ... the most mysterious and poetic – the very symbol of a garden tangle'. Certainly, it was one of his most successful pieces. There is a pleasing interplay between the depictions of the flower at different stages of its development – just opening out and in full bloom – and these are bound together by a host of other details, such as fritillaries, poppies and yew twigs.

Honeysuckle was one of Morris's broadest patterns, often requiring the full width of the fabric for the repeat (a full 36 inches on linens and cottons). This never worried Morris, who far preferred expansive designs to those that were densely-packed. 'Do not be afraid of large patterns,' he said; 'if properly designed they are more restful to the eye than small ones: on the whole, a pattern where the structure is large and the details much broken up is the most useful ... very small rooms, as well as very large ones, look better ornamented with large patterns.'

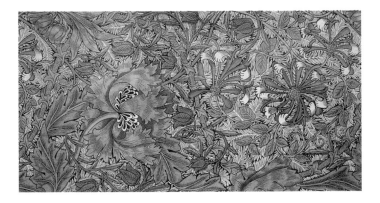

SUNFLOWER COVERLET OR HANGING (C. 1876)

Courtesy of the V&A Picture Library

This striking piece, which was probably intended as a bedcover, is quite different from most of Morris's work. It is the only one of his designs which is known to have been produced by his favourite embroiderer, the talented and highly individual Catherine Holiday. In the main, she worked on designs provided by her husband Henry – an artist and stained-glass painter, probably best remembered for his illustrations in Lewis Carroll's *The Hunting of the Snark* – but she was also employed by Morris on a freelance basis. Whenever he made designs for Catherine, Morris gave her leeway in the way they could be interpreted, which may explain the unusual appearance of this item.

The Firm sold Holiday's work on a commission basis, retaining just 10 per cent of the selling price (a very generous gesture, given that materials were supplied). Despite this, Morris was always concerned that she was pricing herself out of the market – a coverlet could cost as much as £150. His other difficulty was in persuading her to make copies of successful lines. 'I know you don't like doing repetitions,' he said once, 'but this is such a beautiful thing that I should think it a great pity if there were not more than one of it in the world.'

WALLPAPER STAND-BOOK (C. 1905)

Courtesy of the V&A Picture Library

When discussing Morris, there is always a tendency to lay undue emphasis on his wealthiest clients and his grandest decorative schemes. As a socialist, he was well aware of this dichotomy and wanted his work to be available to all, but knew that only the well-off would be able to afford his finest products. In his Oxford Street showroom, which was opened in 1877, he went some way towards countering this. Many smaller items were sold there, including such things as embroidered bags, bell-pulls, photograph frames and even tea cosies. Nevertheless, the main aim of the premises was to show the full range of the Firm's goods. An official brochure was produced, reminding customers that 'it is only in our Show Room, 449 Oxford Street, that they [the goods] can be seen together in such a way that one can support the other ... and so give a true idea of the decoration that we recommend'. There were, in addition, sample-books for all the textile and wallpaper patterns. The pictured example is the larger of the two wallpaper books, containing 132 different patterns. There was also a smaller 'table book', which potential customers could borrow and peruse at their leisure.

THESE PAPERS ARE
PRINTED BY HAND

Hand or Block-printed Papers and Machine-printed Papers.

MORRIS AND COMPANY are often asked "What is the advantage of hand-printed papers over those printed by machine?"

HAND-PRINTED PAPERS are produced very slowly, each block used being dipped into pigment and then firmly pressed on to the paper, giving a great body of colour. This process takes place with each separate colour, which is slowly dried before another is applied. The consequence is that in the finished paper there is a considerable mass of solid colour.

MACHINE-PRINTED PAPERS are produced at a great speed, all the colours being printed at one time and rapidly dried in a heated gallery. In consequence of the speed at which they are printed, there is merely a film of colour deposited on the surface of the paper.

FOR PERMANENT USE we strongly recommend the hand-printed papers.

The machine-printed papers are placed at the end of one of the books or in a small book by themselves.

Show Rooms:
449, Oxford Street, London, W.

MORRIS & Cº TREE FRIE

DO NOT CUT PATTERNS,
QUOTE NAME & NUMBER.

VELVETEEN SAMPLE BOOK (1890s)

Courtesy of the V&A Picture Library

Morris was always swift to react to new trends. In 1877, he noted the rising fashion for printed velveteens and wrote to Wardle, 'we could have a good trade in velvets and serges if we could get the colours good and fast.' The Firm displayed samples of this fabric at the 1888 Arts and Crafts Exhibition, and produced a number of small pattern books. This example features just six designs – *Acanthus*, *Cherwell*, *Florence*, *Wey*, *Severn* and *Mole* – in a variety of different shades. They were produced over a wide period of time, ranging from 1876 to 1892. It is also possible that the Firm used these sample books as a means of testing the market. The Mole design, for example, is only known from two pattern books, and there is nothing to suggest that it was ever put into commercial production.

The warning on the left-hand page offers a salutary reminder about the disadvantages of success. Morris was perhaps the first designer to achieve a recognisable 'look' which was familiar to a wide spectrum of potential clients. Because of this, his designs were pirated on both sides of the Atlantic.

STRAWBERRY THIEF (1883)

Courtesy of the V&A Picture Library

The gentle humour in this pattern helped to make it one of Morris's most successful creations. It was inspired by a real-life problem – one which will be familiar to many gardeners. In his garden at Kelmscott Manor, Morris tried to grow strawberries, but found that these were always being eaten by greedy thrushes who managed to creep under the netting. May Morris recalled: 'you can picture my father going out in the early morning and watching the rascally thrushes at work on the fruitbeds, and telling the gardener, who growls "I'd like to wring their necks!", that no bird in the garden must be touched.' Morris did not attempt to draw the birds himself, but passed this duty across to Philip Webb.

Quite apart from the thrushes, the printing of this pattern caused the artist endless headaches. He was experimenting with new techniques and was not sure how the results would turn out. He was particularly worried about the way that the reds would appear and, as always, felt obliged to take personal charge. 'The colour mixer Kenyon is a good fellow,' he told his daughter Jenny, 'but he is rather a muddler and ... either Wardle or I have to stand over him all the time.'

THE ADORATION OF THE MAGI
(1887–1906)
Courtesy of Norfolk Museums Service

Morris recognised this magnificent tapestry as 'the most important piece I have yet done'. His view was shared by many others, for at least 10 copies are known to have been ordered. The illustrated example dates from 1906, when it was made for the Colman family of Norwich. Apart from the border, it is identical to the original version.

The original commission came from Exeter College in Oxford, where Morris and Burne-Jones had both been students. The weaving took over two years (1888–90) and the college was eventually charged £525. The unusual composition is thoroughly Pre-Raphaelite in character. There is no attempt to create an eastern atmosphere. Instead, Bethlehem is relocated to the edge of a very English wood. The Virgin sits under a thatched canopy, next to a rose bower (her traditional symbol). Beside her, Joseph is portrayed as a genuine woodcutter, with an axe at his feet. To the right, an angel hovers just above the ground, holding the star that guided the Magi to this spot. The figures are by Burne-Jones, who later produced a painted version of the subject called *The Star of Bethlehem*, the flowers are by Dearle and the remaining decoration is the work of Morris.

THE ORCHARD (THE SEASONS) (1890)

Courtesy of the V&A Picture Library

This tapestry is unusual, in that Morris designed the figures as well as the background details. Dearle reported: 'The colouring as well as the general design are by Mr Morris and parts of the figures have been woven by his own hand.' According to reports, Morris borrowed the figures from an earlier project at Jesus College, Cambridge (1866). This had been one of the Firm's most acrimonious commissions – the Dean took umbrage when he discovered that Morris had subcontracted out part of the work – and the artist was eventually bullied into taking personal charge of a row of angels on the chapel ceiling. Morris, who was never fond of working on figures, was clearly determined to gain as much mileage from these angels as possible.

In fact, Morris's approach in *The Orchard* was very similar to that in the *Minstrel* series. He simply removed the angels' wings and then changed the inscription. Whereas the scroll at Jesus College had contained a hymn, the inscription here is taken from one of Morris's own poems. Despite all his efforts, the tapestry proved hard to sell and no copies were ever commissioned.

THE GREEN DINING ROOM (1866–67)

Courtesy of the V&A Picture Library

In the mid-1860s, the Firm received two highly prestigious commissions, which signalled just how impressive their reputation had become. The first of these contracts came from St James's Palace, where Morris's men were asked to refurbish the Tapestry Room and Armoury. The second came from the South Kensington Museum, where they were hired to design a public dining room. The latter was the brainchild of the museum's progressive director, Henry Cole, who was determined that his workplace should itself be a thing of beauty. The room, which survives in its original state, is no longer used for dining purposes and is now called the William Morris Room. Some items of furniture produced by the Firm are usually on display there.

Within the room, Morris and his associates strove to create an air of medieval sumptuousness. The general design is largely by Webb, who was also responsible for the panelling, the gesso wall decoration and much of the ceiling. Burne-Jones designed the stained glass and the gilded panels, which took as their theme the months of the year. The upper frieze, also by Webb, depicts a series of dogs running after hares. These are said to have been inspired by the font at Newcastle Cathedral.

CEILING DESIGN (C. 1866)

Courtesy of the V&A Picture Library

This is one of the many surviving preparatory designs for the Green Dining Room at the South Kensington Museum. It shows part of the pattern used on the ceiling, which was jointly conceived by Morris and Webb. Not surprisingly, Morris's drawings concentrated on interweaving strands of foliage, while Webb's contributions were more geometric and controlled.

While Morris clearly enjoyed taking part in the design process, his chief function at South Kensington was to supervise the overall project. In this area, the members of the Firm were still on a steep learning curve and their inexperience showed in two key areas – drawing up estimates and managing the workforce. Morris was anxious to be fair in his commercial dealings and, before the dining room commission, had invariably underpriced his estimates. He would often operate on an unrealistic profit margin of just five per cent. The estimates at South Kensington included £272 for the stained glass, £277 for the dado and ceiling, and just over £291 for the various painted panels. Morris's other duty was to instruct and supervise the workmen involved on the project. In addition to the Firm's employees, he also used a few outside contractors. At South Kensington, for example, he hired the firm of Dunn & Co. to carry out some of the decorating.

CEILING DESIGN (C. 1866)

Courtesy of the V&A Picture Library

This charcoal and watercolour sketch is one of Philip Webb's designs for the Green Dining Room at the South Kensington Museum. It shows the decorative detail around the edges of the large roundels, which filled the central panel of the ceiling. It is close, but not identical, to the design that was eventually selected. The sheet is marked with a few paint splatters, which may mean that it was used on site anyway.

Details of the execution of the decoration have been thoroughly documented. Webb charged the Firm £7 for completed designs and £1 3 shillings for his visits to monitor the progress of the plasterwork. Once the plastering was finished, it took one of the workmen two-and-a-half days to trace out and prick the design on to the ceiling. Next, the basic outline of the pattern was painted in – a job that took four men two days – and this was then worked up into its finished state at a rate of four-and-a-half square feet per day. Work was intensive and one man was employed full-time simply to mix the colours. The cost of the execution of this section of the commission was calculated at £86 16 shillings, based on an estimate of a single man employed for 243 days.

DESIGN FOR ST JAMES'S WALLPAPER (1880)

Courtesy of the William Morris Gallery

This original design, executed in pencil and a sepia wash, is dated 23 July 1880. Just one week earlier, Morris had met officials from the Board of Works, to discuss the details of a new commission from St James's Palace. After the meeting, he wasted no time in drawing up plans for a new wallpaper, specifically designed for this prestigious job. Fittingly, the *St James's* was large and grandiose, dominated by a sweep of acanthus leaves. It was eventually used in a combination of delicate pastel shades on the Grand Staircase, the Queen's Staircase and the Ambassadors' Staircase. A more lavish version of the pattern, in red silk damask, was used in the Throne Room. Morris also created the *Oak* design for this commission. The work was completed in three stages between 1880 and 1882.

The Firm undertook two major schemes of redecoration at St James's Palace (the first had been carried out in 1866–67). They owed these opportunities to the magnetic charm of Dante Gabriel Rossetti. He used his contacts to approach William Cowper, First Commissioner of Public Works, and persuaded him of the supreme quality of the Firm's work.

BEDROOM, KELMSCOTT MANOR (C. 1874)

Courtesy of Country Life Picture Library

This is a photograph of Morris's bedroom at Kelmscott Manor in the Cotswolds. It shows most of the original furnishings. The centrepiece, of course, is the huge, seventeenth-century bed, which is roughly contemporary with the house itself. Morris's poem 'On the Bed at Kelmscott' appears as an inscription on the valance. The bed hangings were designed and worked by his daughter May, with the assistance of Ellen Wright and Lily Yeats (sister of W. B. Yeats). The bedcover was embroidered by Jane Morris, and a portrait of her by Rossetti can be seen on the wall behind.

Morris began renting Kelmscott in 1871 although at first he must have had mixed feelings about the place. This was the time of Rossetti's affair with Jane and, between 1871 and 1874, the two of them were living there together, virtually as man and wife. Rossetti even set up a studio in the Tapestry Room. After Rossetti moved out, however, the Manor became Morris's favourite retreat, the place where he could escape from the cares of work and his unhappy marriage. It is no accident that he made it the focus of his socialist dream in *News from Nowhere*.

DESIGN FOR WINDRUSH WALLPAPER (1881–83)

Courtesy of the William Morris Society

Morris produced various different types of design. His preparatory drawings for the *St James's* wallpaper or the ceiling at the South Kensington Museum, for example, were early sketches, in which his main concern was to work out the basic structure of his pattern. The *Windrush* design comes from a later stage in the process. Here, the pattern and the colouring are already clear in his mind, and the purpose of the design is to help the block-cutter and the printer to proceed with their stage of the work. In this particular instance, Morris has made life rather difficult for his cutter by outlining the bare minimum of the design. A distinct design, such as the one for the *Grafton* wallpaper, would have been more helpful.

Windrush, registered in October 1883, was one of Morris's last designs for a printed textile. In common with a number of other patterns from this period – *Kennet, Cray, Evenlode* – it was loosely based on a seventeenth-century velvet in the South Kensington Museum. The design was available in several colours, including a bright, monochrome red. Morris had a *Windrush* hanging in the drawing room at Kelmscott House, using it 'as a summer change'.

DESIGN FOR GRAFTON WALLPAPER (1883)

Courtesy of the William Morris Society

This design illustrates an advanced stage in the design process. The structure of the pattern has been fully worked out and a preferred colour combination selected. The full outline of the pattern has been traced out, ready for the block-cutter, and a generous central portion – more than a single repeat – has been coloured in. *Grafton* wallpaper would eventually be available in a choice of two- or three-colour formats, but this is the three-colour variety, with pale green, yellow and a second green.

At the next stage, the design was transferred on to three separate blocks – one for each of the colours. This was a highly specialised job and one for which Morris employed the well-established firm of Barretts in Bethnal Green. One of the hardest tasks was the cutting away of the unwanted portion of the design on each of the blocks. The cutter's tracing-marks were always submitted to Morris for his approval before this 'rubbing off' process could begin. Not many of the original blocks have survived, but Arthur Sanderson & Sons Ltd still own the three separate carvings for the *Grafton* pattern.

DESIGN FOR JASMINE WALLPAPER (1872)

Courtesy of the V&A Picture Library

This is one of Morris's most intricate wallpaper patterns. More than most, it has a genuine sense of depth. This is provided by the winding tendrils, which knit together the background of hawthorn leaves and tiny blossoms, and the foreground of pale jasmine. There is a firm structure behind the pattern – the flowers are on a diagonal slant and the tendrils form slender, vertical hoops – but this is so well disguised that, at first glance, it gives the impression of an untidy tangle of wild flowers. In this sense, the design represents one of Morris's finest attempts at portraying natural, organic growth.

The production of such a complex pattern was no easy matter. No fewer than four detailed designs have survived, rather more than were usually necessary, and the records from the Firm's printing works suggest that there were considerable teething problems. Apparently, the first version of the design required 20 different colour blocks and, for obvious commercial reasons, attempts were made to reduce this number. Ultimately, though, the popularity of the finished design made this worthwhile. One of the satisfied customers was Burne-Jones, who used *Jasmine* in the drawing room at The Grange, his home in Fulham.

JASMINE AND TRELLIS DESIGN (1868–70)

Courtesy of the V&A Picture Library

This was Morris's first design for a furnishing textile. It is probably no coincidence that, as with his first wallpaper design, he structured the pattern around a trellis. This was an unsubtle device, which gave the finished composition a rather heavy and formulaic appearance, but it did help him ease his way gently into a new area of creativity.

As always when embarking on a different venture, Morris's key decision revolved around the method of production. By the 1860s, most manufacturers were using engraved rollers for their printed textiles, but as so often before, Morris found the modern methods unsatisfactory. After careful consideration, he opted for the centuries-old tradition of block-printing. This was a desperately slow and labour-intensive process – a separate block was required for each colour – but it also had certain advantages. It offered the designer far greater control over his colours and was perfect for short production runs. After a hunt, Morris managed to track down a printworks that had used this method up until the 1840s and was prepared to revert to it. The firm in question was Thomas Clarkson of Preston, who produced the first run of *Jasmine and Trellis* in about 1870. Morris later switched to Thomas Wardle's works.

DESIGN FOR PIMPERNEL WALLPAPER (1876)

Courtesy of the V&A Picture Library

Morris had very firm views on how his clients should select their wallpaper. His philosophy was set out at length in a brochure produced in 1883 when the Firm was exhibiting its wares at the Foreign Fair in Boston. 'In the Decorative Arts,' he began, 'nothing is finally successful which does not satisfy the mind as well as the eye. A pattern may have beautiful parts and be good in certain relations; but, unless it is suitable for the purpose assigned, it will not be a decoration.' He then went on to list his ideas for individual patterns, declaring: 'You must decide for yourself whether the room ... is too stiff and formal ... If too great a rigidity be the fault, choose a pattern with soft easy lines, either boldly circular or oblique wavy – say *Scroll, Vine, Pimpernel, Fruit*.'

Pimpernel falls into the 'boldly circular' category. Although it is hard to gain a true impression of scale from a reproduction, the flower heads are extremely large – in the billiard room at Wightwick, there is only space for a vertical line of six blooms between the picture rail and the dado. Morris followed his own advice and hung the pattern in his dining room at Kelmscott House.

FLOWERPOT DESIGN (C. 1878)

Courtesy of the V&A Picture Library

This is one of a series of small embroidery designs, which Morris created in the late 1870s and early 1880s. These were specifically targeted at customers of modest means, who wanted to own an example of the great man's work but could not afford to redecorate whole rooms in his expensive wares. This particular pattern was used for both firescreen panels and cushion covers. It was available ready-made in the Oxford Street shop, but could also be purchased in kit form. Examples of both the professional and home-made varieties have survived.

The two most accomplished versions of the panel, executed in different colour schemes, were made by Morris's daughter, May. The pictured example was bequeathed by her to the Victoria and Albert Museum. May took over the Firm's embroidery department in 1885, heading a team of other talented needlewomen. In later life, she taught and lectured on the subject, passing on much of her expertise in an influential book, *Decorative Needlework* (1893). In 1907, she also became a founder member of the Women's Guild of Arts. She never moved far from her father's orbit, residing first in Hammersmith Terrace and then moving back to Kelmscott Manor in the Cotswolds where she lived until her death in 1938.

DESIGN FOR VINE WALLPAPER (1875)

Courtesy of Christie's Images

The *Vine* pattern was registered in 1874 and was initially available in two colour schemes, 'olive vine' and 'blue vine'. These appeared highly naturalistic, following Morris's advice to his fellow designers that 'no stem should be so far from its parent stock as to look weak and wavering'. He added to this effect by skilfully concealing his repeats through a discreet meandering pattern. This obeyed one of his other favourite maxims, namely that 'the more mysteriously you interweave your sprays and stems the better'.

After the success of the early issues, Morris decided to bring out a more luxurious version of the design. The pictured example was first produced in 1875, using oil colours and lacquered paper. Its rich golden hues, which positively glow when seen on a broad expanse of wall, certainly created the desired air of opulence, but customers had to pay a high price for it. A single roll retailed at 40 shillings while the earlier format sold for just 12 shillings. At the other end of the scale, Morris made use of the background block from *Vine* to produce another wallpaper pattern entitled *Willow*.

WANDLE DESIGN FOR TEXTILE (1884)

Courtesy of the V&A Picture Library

Together with *Cray*, this was one of Morris's most intricate and expensive patterns. It was also another in his series of 'river' chintzes. This particular tributary, however, which also gave its name to the borough of Wandsworth, had a very special significance for Morris. The Firm's works at Merton Abbey were located on its banks and all its cottons were washed in the river, prior to printing. While he was busy with the initial design, Morris wrote to his daughter Jenny explaining, 'if it succeeds I shall call it *Wandle*: the connection may not seem obvious to you as the wet Wandle is not big but small, but you see it will have to be very elaborate to honour our helpful stream...'

The pattern displays a strong, diagonal meander, mimicking the winding course of a river. In common with the other designs in the series, Morris drew his inspiration from a seventeenth-century Italian velvet, which he had seen at the South Kensington Museum shortly after its acquisition in 1883. Unlike the others, however, the brightly coloured stripes add a rather jaunty air to the finished design.

ACANTHUS COVERLET OR HANGING
(C. 1880)

Courtesy of the V&A Picture Library

Throughout his career, Morris was fascinated by the pattern-making possibilities of the acanthus leaf. When curled up tight, it could form a dense, mysterious background, as it does in his wallpaper pattern and in tapestries such as *The Forest* or *The Woodpecker*. Here, however, it is flattened out and used as a linking device, binding together the bright array of tiny blooms in the central panel and the border.

This hanging dates from the period when Morris was teaching himself to weave and was attempting to introduce carpet-making into the Firm's repertoire. The influence of the latter is clearly evident here for, at first glance, the quartered design appears far more typical of a carpet than a hanging. In spite of this, *Acanthus* proved to be one of Morris's most popular embroidery designs. Quite a few copies are known to have survived, although the finest of these is certainly the pictured example by May Morris, which confirms her astonishing gifts as a colourist. Another example, also housed at the Victoria and Albert Museum, was produced by Lady Bell and her daughters for Rounton Grange, their home in Northallerton, Yorkshire.

ACANTHUS SAMPLE HANGING (C. 1880)

Courtesy of the V&A Picture Library

Embroidery had been one of Morris's earliest interests, dating back to his enthusiastic decoration of the Red House in the early 1860s. By the end of the following decade, however, his energies were increasingly being diverted into other projects, such as weaving and carpet-making, which were becoming his main priorities. This, in turn, meant that he produced fewer new designs. By the early 1880s, these fell into two broad categories: small designs intended for use as firescreens or cushion covers (the four main examples of these were *Flowerpot*, *Rose Wreath*, *Rosebush* and *Clanfield*); and larger and more intricate patterns, based around a single, central motif. The latter reflected the artist's growing interest in carpet design.

Sales of the large embroideries were encouraging but, with Morris occupied elsewhere, managers of the Firm found it difficult to meet the demand for new designs. One solution was to produce variations of the most popular lines. The *Acanthus* hanging, for example, had four known variants. The most unusual is this small version, which reproduces about a quarter of the original design. Opinion is divided as to whether this was a clumsy attempt to breathe new life into an old design, or whether it was simply meant as a sample, illustrating different borders and motifs in the Firm's repertoire.

TULIP AND WILLOW DESIGN FOR TEXTILE (1873)

Courtesy of Birmingham Museums and Art Gallery

This highly finished design was for Morris's second textile pattern, which was registered in December 1873. As he had been satisfied with Thomas Clarkson's handling of its predecessor, he sent it up to Preston to be printed. This time he was horrified by the results. Instead of using a genuine shade of indigo, Clarkson printed the design in a brash Prussian blue, the nearest to indigo that could be achieved using modern aniline dyes. This led Morris to speak out against the capitalist forces which he considered had brought his industry to such a parlous state. 'Henceforward there is an absolute divorce between the commercial process and the art of printing. Anyone wanting to produce dyed textiles with any artistic quality in them must entirely forgo the modern and commercial methods in favour of those which are at least as old as Pliny...'

In practical terms, Morris severed his connection with Clarkson and abandoned production of *Tulip and Willow*. He also set up a tiny dyehouse in the basement and scullery of his house in Queen Square, hoping that he might find his own solution to the problem. In fact it was only in 1883, after he had established himself at Merton Abbey, that he was finally able to produce a satisfactory printing of *Tulip and Willow*.

TULIP DESIGN FOR TEXTILE (1875)

Courtesy of the V&A Picture Library

Tulip was the first of Morris's designs to be printed by Thomas Wardle of Leek in Staffordshire, following Morris's disastrous experience with Thomas Clarkson in 1873. Morris had initially made contact with Wardle through his brother-in-law, George Wardle, who was a manager with the Firm. Thomas had been running his own printing and dyeing business for the past five years but – more interestingly from Morris's point of view – he had a grounding in older techniques. This came from his father, Joshua, a prominent silk dyer in the 1840s.

The first results of the new business relationship were promising enough for, by 1878, Wardle was printing no fewer than 14 of the Firm's designs. The first four of these – *Marigold, Larkspur, Tulip* and *Carnation* – were all quite similar in format and were closely related to Morris's wallpaper designs. Despite this encouraging start, Morris's dealings with Wardle became soured over the course of the next few years. By the early 1880s, the standard of the latter's printing had deteriorated, causing Morris to write, 'I laboured hard on making good designs for these and on getting good colour: they are now so printed and coloured that they are no better than caricatures of my careful work.'